Professor Ch'u Chai is eminently qualified to tell "the story of Chinese philosophy." Educated in China and the United States, he was formerly a professor at the Universities of Nanking and Taiwan, and both a dean and a professor at the Law College of the National University at Chungking. At present, he is Professor of Chinese Culture and Philosophy at the New School for Social Research.

In addition to his teaching, he is widely known and respected as the author of numerous articles and books both in English and Chinese.

His purpose in this book has been to inform the layman on a subject that has too long been reserved for the serious student. To that end, Professor Chai has included a helpful glossary, and he has personally translated all original writings into English that is as clear and lucid as possible.

The story of
CHINESE PHILOSOPHY

Ch'u Chai with Winberg Chai

WASHINGTON SQUARE PRESS, INC. • NEW YORK

THE STORY OF
CHINESE PHILOSOPHY

1961

L

Published by
Washington Square Press, Inc.: Executive Offices, 630 Fifth Avenue;
University Press Division, 32 Washington Place, New York, N.Y.

WASHINGTON SQUARE PRESS editions are distributed in the U.S. by
Affiliated Publishers, Inc., 630 Fifth Avenue, New York 20, N.Y.

Copyright, ©, 1961, by Washington Square Press, Inc. All rights reserved. Published on the same day in Canada by Washington Square Press, Inc. Printed in the U.S.A.

TO

HUNTINGTON CAIRNS

Acknowledgment

I wish to express my appreciation to my son, Winberg Chai, a member of the New School faculty, for his collaboration in the writing of this book. As this work has progressed over the past five years, I have also benefited from various discussions with many of my colleagues and students at the New School. In particular, my gratitude goes to Dr. Alvin Johnson, President-Emeritus of the New School, and Dean Clara Mayer of the philosophy and liberal arts faculty, for their support and encouragement.

I should also like to thank Eugene J. Prakapas of Washington Square Press, Inc., himself a trained scholar at Oxford, who not only edited the manuscript with rare thoroughness and perception but also helped clarify many basic questions of substance; and Mr. Freeman Lewis, for his many kindnesses. I am also indebted to Yao Kuo-liang, head of the art department of the National Historical Museum, in Taiwan, for the beautiful illustrations included in this book.

I am especially grateful to many of my friends and former colleagues in Taiwan, who sent me the necessary materials for the compilation of this book. I regret that the high cost of printing the Chinese makes it impossible to add here a bibliography of the Chinese works that I have used.

Last but not least, my thanks are due to my wife, without whose patience and encouragement this book could not have become a possibility.

CH'U CHAI

New School for Social Research
New York City

Contents

INTRODUCTION	xiii
1. Confucius	1
2. Mencius	41
3. Lao Tzŭ	69
4. Chuang Tzŭ	93
5. Yang Chu	113
6. Mo Tzŭ	127
7. Hsün Tzŭ	161
8. Han Fei Tzŭ	195
CONCLUSION: Chinese Philosophy over the Ages	225
GLOSSARY	239
SELECTED BIBLIOGRAPHY	247

The Story of
Chinese Philosophy

Introduction

The Scope and Structure of This Book

This book is designed to serve the layman as a readable, nontechnical introduction to a fascinating but complex field.

An introductory discussion characterizes the Chinese way of thought so as to enable the average reader to bridge the gap between the Oriental and Western minds. In addition, a brief account is given of the origins and beginnings of Chinese philosophy.

The body of the book consists of eight chapters, each devoted to one of the gigantic figures who dominate the field of Chinese philosophy. Since the intention is a layman's introduction to the entire field, the emphasis is upon the philosophers themselves rather than upon any extended analysis of their teachings. Specifically, the following outline governs each chapter:

1. A biographical sketch of the philosopher concerned.
2. A discussion of his teachings stressing the most important characteristics.

3. A consideration of social and political influences acting upon the philosopher and his outlooks.
4. A comparison with the other great philosophers —how the various sages rivaled yet complemented each other; how they employed ideas and writings of the past and of each other.
5. An estimate of the influence of the philosopher under discussion upon the development of the Chinese mind.

Each chapter is a separate unit that can be read without reference to the rest of the book. However, the reader is encouraged to begin with the first chapter and then move on page by page so as to grasp the close relationship between all these figures.

Finally, Chinese philosophy is traced over the ages in such a way as to suggest at least some of the influences that have contributed to the making of the contemporary Chinese mind.

Translation of technical philosophical terms is extremely difficult. For many of the Chinese terms only approximately equivalent terms can be found in English. Hence, translation must often be accompanied by interpretation, if the meaning is to be grasped by Western readers. While special effort has been made to translate these terms in the clearest possible way, it should be remembered that many of the most profound as well as the most difficult human conceptions are to be found in Chinese philosophy. Moreover, a single Chinese character often condenses the meaning of many English words. Then, too, such philosophical ideas are difficult in themselves, however lucidly translated and interpreted. For added clarity, a glossary has been included to suggest the equivalence between important Chinese terms and their Western counterparts.

Another difficulty involves the sources of Chinese philosophical literature. Hu Shih, in his *The Development of Logical Method in Ancient China*, has pointed out:

> Of philosophical literature of the period extending from the death of Confucius (479 B.C.) to the last quarter of the fourth century B.C. very little reliable source material has come down to us.

The reason for this lack of earlier literature is largely the "fire of Ch'in," (213 B.C.), which resulted in an incalculable loss to Chinese literature. Hence, our knowledge of the ancient documents is the result of the laborious sifting by scholars of lost books from their ashes.

It should be added that although the treatment of subject matter in this book may be said to be a novel experiment, no pretense is made that it is exhaustive or that all the arguments and points of emphasis are original.

Throughout these pages, the interests of the general reader have been the main consideration. An extensive bibliography has been included for the use of those who may wish to pursue this field more deeply.

The Nature of Chinese Philosophy

Certain underlying principles serve to distinguish Chinese from Western philosophy.

In the first place, whereas Western philosophy is associated with science and religion, Chinese is closer to ethics, politics, literature and the arts. This is because the ideal of knowledge for its own sake is not to be found in China, where knowledge is desired merely as a means to applied and noble ends. Science, as Plato and Aristotle said, has roots in wonder, in the desire to know and understand for the sole sake of knowing and understanding. But the roots of Chinese thought lie in the anxiety of the sages to "understand the ways of nature and know the needs of the people."[1] This is not a scientific but a practical spirit, which emphasizes the moral qualities of man rather than his intellectual capacities. Hence, Chinese philosophy has from the outset failed to lay the foundations for science. It is conceivable that China, with her early development of culture and her noteworthy inventions in industry, might have developed the sciences more extensively and fruitfully than she has. But this practical and ethical way of thinking has been the big obstacle to such development. Taoist mysticism is the only exception here. Taoist alchemy, in its pursuit of the philosopher's stone and the elixir of life, was the source of pseudo-chemistry; and Taoist Yoga, with its emphasis on meditation and breathing

---

[1] *Yi Ching*, Appendix III, I-72.

exercises, teaches how to alleviate disease and prolong life. Also, Taoist mysticism generally has the spirit of science, but its teachings have never been explored very much from this standpoint.

Again, in contrast to Westerners, the Chinese are not intense in religion. Each great Chinese system of thought developed primarily as a philosophy of self-cultivation and only incidentally as a religious cult. Most Chinese philosophers have denied the elements that, to Westerners, distinguish religion from mere philosophy: first, a belief in a Supreme Being; second, a belief in the immortality of the soul. Of all the great philosophers of the Chou period, Mo Tzŭ was the only one who believed in Heaven as the Divine Being, and even he used this belief merely as a motivating force for his essentially humanistic doctrine of all-embracing love. Thus, where the Westerner is religious and basically concerned with love for God, the Chinese is humanistic and ethical, occupied mainly with social relations, civil duties and moral codes.

Chinese philosophy also differs from Western philosophy in method and attitude of study. Professor F. S. C. Northrop has defined this in his distinction between two major types of concepts, one achieved by intuition and the other by postulation:

A concept of intuition is one which denotes and the complete meaning of which is given by something that is immediately apprehended. . . . A concept of postulation is one the complete meaning of which is designated by the postulates of the deductive theory in which it occurs.[2]

The first of these concepts characterizes Chinese philosophy, with its stress on meditation and methods of self-cultivation resulting in a deep preoccupation with concrete problems and a distaste for the abstract. The second is true of Western thought and its qualities of speculation and logical analysis. This Chinese disposition has naturally enriched intuitive understanding but paralyzed logical reasoning and abstract generalization. The inevitable by-product of this has been an almost total absence of experimental procedures. Confucius once said:

> Let us teach the way to knowledge. Only say that you know when you really know, and concede your ignorance of what you do not know—this is the way to knowledge.[3]

Such an ideal definition of the limits of one's knowledge may seem impossible to the Western mind, but when viewed in light of the above distinction, it can be seen as a natural goal for the Chinese, unconcerned with limitless speculation.

Western and Chinese philosophy further differ in their contents. Western is generally divided into five fields of study: logic, the study of method; aesthetics,

---

[2] "The Contemporary Emphasis of Eastern Intuitive Philosophy and Western Scientific Philosophy," *Philosophy, East and West*, C. A. Moore, ed. Princeton: Princeton University Press, 1944, pp. 168-234.

[3] *Analects*, II-17.

the study of beauty; ethics, the study of conduct; politics, the study of government and social institutions; and metaphysics, the study of being. Chinese philosophy, however, has seldom separated itself from ethical and practical needs. This does not mean that logic, aesthetics and metaphysics are absent; rather it is simply that they are connected with the ethical and practical in one way or another. This factor is yet another result of their concern with human relations and morality.

Finally, the two differ in their fundamental spirit. Western philosophy is impressed by the antagonism of the different factors of the world: the antagonism of human versus divine, of ideal versus real, of society versus individual, of authority versus liberty and so forth. But Chinese philosophy is marked not by antagonism but by the continuity of the world. To the Chinese, for instance, man is part of the universe, and the universe is part of man's being. At any moment in our existence, our life and nature are inextricably intertwined and completely involved in each other. This is the theory of the unity of Heaven and man as enunciated by Confucian scholars; it is also the doctrine of "the equalization of all things" advocated by the great Taoist philosopher Chuang Tzŭ.

The essence of Chinese philosophy resides in its apprehension of total synthesis, which is called the *Tao*. For instance, *yin* and *yang*, the passive female and the active male principles in Chinese philosophy, may be likened to thesis and antithesis in Western philosophy. However, the interplay of *yin* and *yang* does not portray two antagonistic forces but two complementary facets of this *Tao*—instead of opposition, there is co-operation. Again, in the Taoist system, the distinction between *yu* and *wu* is as great as that between being and nonbeing in Greek philosophy. *Yu* and *wu*, however, do not represent opposite concepts; instead, they denote two stages of creation which, though bearing different names, have a common origin—the *Tao*.

Above all, Chinese philosophy is a blend of the idealistic and realistic, the ethical yet metaphysical. This is largely due to the clash between the two major systems of Chinese thought, Taoism and Confucianism. The former in its mystic and otherworldly outlook has ever contended with the very down-to-earth humanism of Confucianism. This struggle over the centuries has produced a situation where, finally, these schools complement each other in a confident balance between extremes.

It is this spirit of synthesis that must be borne in mind if Chinese philosophy is to be understood.

The Origins of Chinese Philosophy

The two mainstreams of Chinese thought have been Confucianism and Taoism, founded in the sixth century B.C. by Confucius and Lao Tzŭ respectively. However, in spite of their importance and their early date, they do not properly represent the origins of Chinese philosophy since both Confucius and Lao Tzŭ are known to have used important classics of earlier times in their study.

Of the ancient works, possibly the true cradle of Chinese philosophy is the *Pa Kua* or "Eight Trigrams," consisting of various combinations of straight lines arranged in a circle. Supposedly, these were evolved from the markings on the shell of a tortoise by Fu Hsi, one of the mythical emperors of antiquity (see Diagram I). They consisted of two primary forms: a continuous straight line (———) called *yang-yao*, or the symbol of the male or positive principle; and a broken line (— —) called *yin-yao*, or the symbol of the female or negative principle. Tradition asserts that these trigrams first received systematic treatment at the hands of King Wên, founder of the Chou dynasty, and his son, the Duke of Chou, and that they then became the basis of metaphysics and occultism as set forth in the *Yi Ching* or *Book of Changes*.

The Eight Trigrams symbolized the eight fundamental elements or factors of the universe (Heaven, Earth, Thunder, Water, Mountain, Wind, Fire, Marshes) and the different abstract attributes that would be suggested and associated with them. Later, the Eight Trigrams were combined until there were Sixty-four Hexagrams—each supposed to symbolize one or more phenomena of the universe, either natural or human. Together, the hexagrams were supposed to represent symbolically all that had happened in the universe.

The importance of these symbols cannot be overemphasized. Before the time of Confucius, the sacred book containing them, commonly known as the *Yi*, was used for divination and for explaining natural

DIAGRAM I—The Eight Trigrams with the symbol of creation in the center

phenomena as well as the complexity of human affairs. Even later, Confucians and Taoists all used the *Yi* to express their ideas, and it served as a bridge between the teachings of the opposing schools.

The other early work of monumental import was the *Shu Ching* or *Book of History*. The documents of which this work was originally composed are said to have numbered one hundred, covering a period of sixteen centuries (2400–800 B.C.). These are the best historical documents in existence for the study of ancient Chinese history, politics and thought.

One remark must be made about the origins of Chinese philosophy apart from such essentially historical considerations. Western philosophy is by and large a product of Greece of the sixth century B.C. In their early days, the Greeks of the mainland migrated to the nearby islands of the Aegean and to Sicily, Southern Italy, Asia Minor—in short, almost to the limits of the then known world. Incidental to this process was a natural development of curiosity about the universe and man's role in it, really a search after the facts and laws of nature. This led to an interaction between philosophy and science so that the greatest philosophers were at the same time men of science: Pythagoras, Plato and Aristotle.

The situation in ancient China was different, for China lies in the center of the great land mass of Eastern Asia, occupying a vast area that naturally felt no need for outside exploration. It is not surprising to find the world of man more important to the ancient Chinese than the world of nature. Their thought was focused on social and political problems instead of the scientific, with the result that where the Greeks were scientists and philosophers, the Chinese were political theoreticians and philosophers. This interest in social and political institutions, as inaugurated by the early sage-kings, though they had not yet constructed a proper system of philosophy, is what lends special significance to the *Shu Ching* or *Book of History*. It is this area of interest that is the real starting point of Chinese philosophy.

The Classical Age of Chinese Philosophy

The Chou period (1122–256 B.C.) is known to historians of Chinese culture as the Classical Age. It is comparable to the Golden Age of Greece because, like its Western counterpart, it established the cultural norms for its society. All succeeding Chinese philosophy is based upon the teachings of the great philosophers of the Chou period.

About 900 B.C. the feudal empire of Chou began to show symptoms of decay. The princes of individual feudal states were becoming strong, and by constant warfare a number of the weaker states were eliminated. The remaining strong states defied the authority of the Chou house. At the instigation of the princes, if not with their actual assistance, semicivilized tribesmen from western China defeated the Chou overlord and overran the royal domain in modern Shansi Province, near Sian. And in 771 B.C., the Chous moved their capital east to the city of Loyi, modern Loyang, in Honan, and the dynasty was afterwards known as the East Chou. Then came the Ch'un Ch'iu (Spring and Autumn) era (722–481 B.C.), which was followed by the Chan-Kuo or Age of Warring States (480–222 B.C.), with the states playing a dominant role while the overlord was reduced to a figurehead.

The entire period was one of intense political,

social and intellectual activity, during which all established conventions and institutions came in for destructive criticism. The conditions of the time were so decidedly unsatisfactory that criticism and protest developed to the sophisticated point where they became schools of thought. The birth of this critical sense in the Chinese people was the awakening of what in Europe in the eighteenth century was called the modern spirit, the spirit of liberalism, the spirit of inquiry. This "modern" spirit in China spread a variety of original ideas. The Chinese mind, hitherto long confined to tradition, seemed suddenly to burst forth from its bonds and riot in the new freedom. Men were free to look anew from any angle they chose and to draw whatever conclusions they liked. It was this freedom that resulted in the greatest intellectual movement ever known in China.

The period from the sixth through the third centuries B.C. saw the flowering of ancient Chinese philosophy and gave rise to the so-called Hundred (i.e., sundry or various) Schools of thought, among which Confucianism and Taoism were two very important ones. The Hundred Schools have generally been classified into six major schools of thought: the Tao Chia, or Taoist School (Taoism); the Ju Chia, or School of Literati (Confucianism); the Mo Chia, or Mohist School (Mohism); the Fa Chia, or Legalist School (Legalism); the Yin-Yang Chia, or Yin-Yang School (Occultism); and the Ming Chia, or School of Names (Sophism). Of the six, only the first four have made a lasting contribution. The Yin-Yang School and the School of Names cannot make such claims although they provided a rich field for scientific research and discoveries. The Yin-Yang School was an offshoot of the Taoist, believing in the existence of *yin* (female) and *yang* (male) as two cosmic principles by whose interaction all changes in the universe were produced. It was also known as the Wu Hsing (Five Elements) School because of its theory that each period of history was dominated by one of the five elements: earth, wood, metal, fire and water. All its writings have perished, and it later became associated with occult matters, magic and charms and failed to develop an independent system of thought. The School of Names evolved from the Mohist School, and its members were a group of Sophists and dialecticians. They became politicians versed in the art of speech, but they could not claim to be philosophers.

Thus, in terms of significant influence upon Chinese life, four main systems of thought comprise the general field of Chinese philosophy: Confucianism, Mohism, Taoism and Legalism. These systems are represented by the eight great philosophers of the Chou period: Lao Tzŭ, Confucius, Mo Tzŭ, Yang Chu, Mencius, Chuang Tzŭ, Hsün Tzŭ and Han Fei Tzŭ. All others were merely offshoots from these four mainstreams of thought and their spokesmen (see Diagram II). Each of these eight figures can best be considered in terms of the form of his reaction to the unhappiness of the times.

Lao Tzŭ and his followers concluded that the chaos of the age was proof of something radically wrong in the very nature and constitution of society and civilization. Man had had a paradise, but he had lost it through his own mistakes, which consisted largely of efforts to build an artificial civilization. Hence, man's only solution was to retreat from this civilization to the primitive time—from the state of culture to that of nature. This naturalistic way of thought represents Taoism, which is elaborated in some detail in Chapter 3.

Although Taoists were united in their general ideal of withdrawal, within their own ranks two different interpretations arose of the fundamental concept—the *Tao*—which Lao Tzŭ had made the motivating force of the universe. One view, as represented by Chuang Tzŭ (Chapter 4), considered *Tao* as the totality of spontaneity of all things in the universe, a force or idea that left all things to develop by themselves, naturally and spontaneously. This view can be classified as the idealistic or romantic version of Taoism.

On the other hand, Yang Chu (Chapter 5) thought that the *Tao* was a blind physical force, which produced the world not by design or will but by necessity or chance. This view represents hedonism or the materialistic aspect of Taoism.

Another reaction—and probably the most influential—to the turmoil of the period was that characterized by the thought of Confucius and his followers. In contrast to the Taoists, they advocated not withdrawal but a return to the disciplined ceremony and culture of the early Chou period. Confucius' achievement (Chapter 1) lay along these lines: He was the one to transmit the ancient Chinese classics to

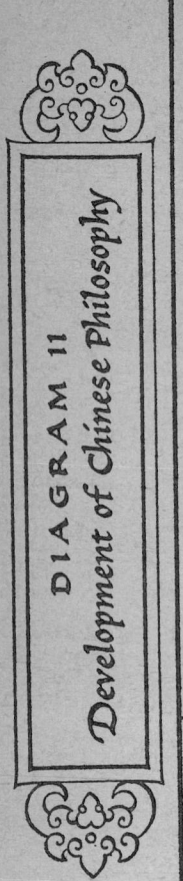

DIAGRAM II
Development of Chinese Philosophy

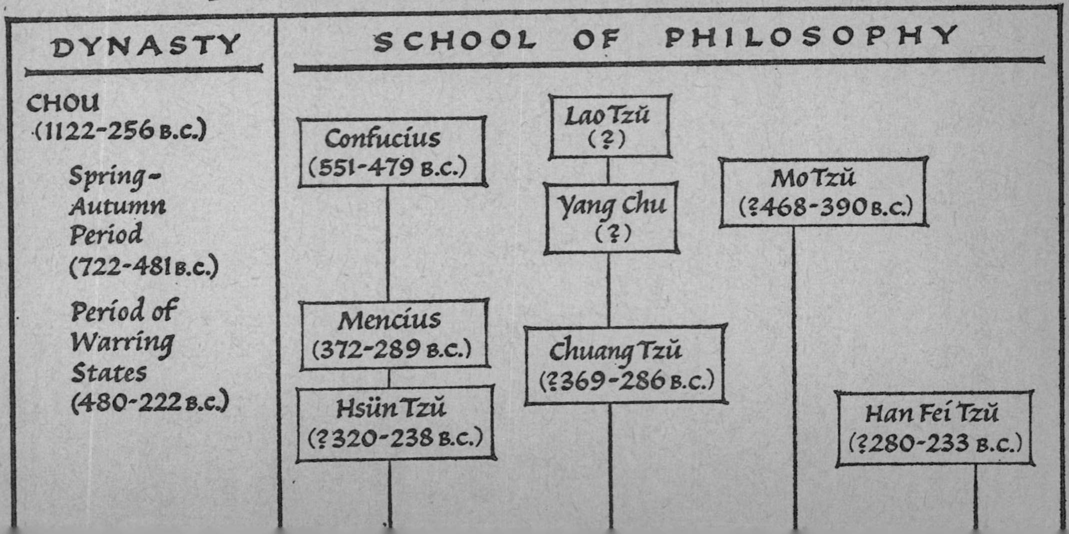

DYNASTY	SCHOOL OF PHILOSOPHY			
CHOU (1122–256 B.C.)				
Spring-Autumn Period (722–481 B.C.)	Confucius (551–479 B.C.)	Lao Tzŭ (?)		
Period of Warring States (480–222 B.C.)	Mencius (372–289 B.C.)	Yang chu (?)	Mo Tzŭ (?468–390 B.C.)	
	Hsün Tzŭ (?320–238 B.C.)	Chuang Tzŭ (?369–286 B.C.)		Han Fei Tzŭ (?280–233 B.C.)

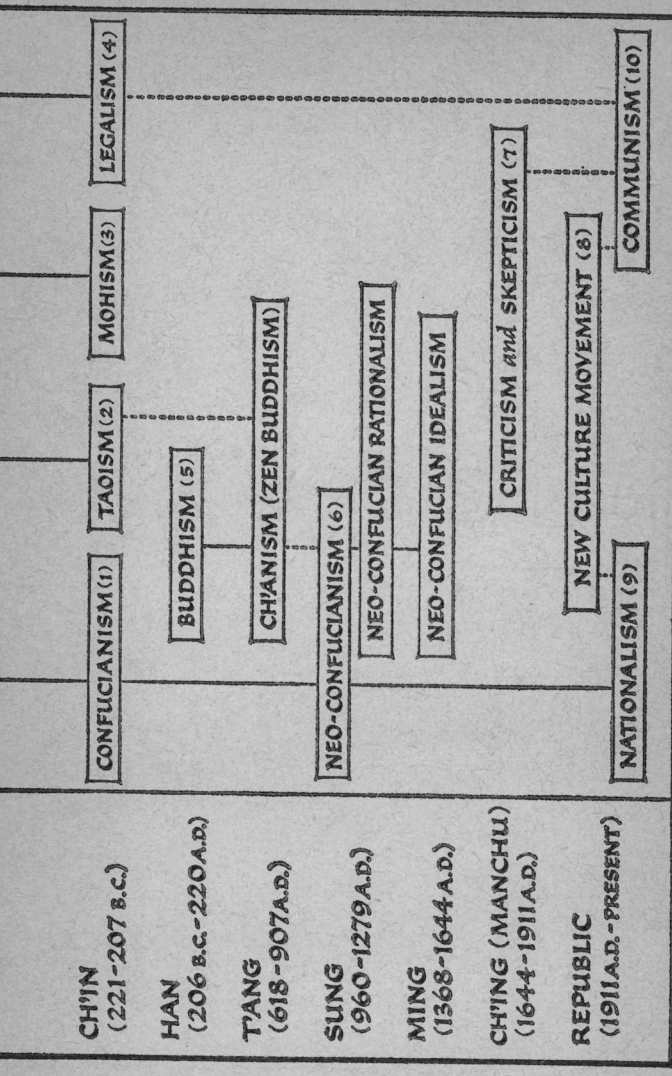

Notes

(1) Confucianism suffered a decline after the time of Mencius. During the Han dynasty (206 B.C.–220 A.D.) it revived and emerged as the state teaching.

(2) Taoism, the chief rival of Confucianism, grew extremely influential in government circles in the early Han period. Its doctrine of *wu wei* was adopted as state policy, and its occultism was accepted as a matter of personal faith.

(3) Mohism failed to revive as a vital philosophy after the "Ch'in fire" (213 B.C.).

(4) Legalism later fell into disgrace because of its connection with the tyrannical rule of the Ch'in dynasty (221–207 B.C.)

(5) Buddhism, which had been introduced from India in the first century A.D., or even earlier, interacted with Taoism and became Chinese Buddhism, evolving as the Ch'an or Zen school.

(6) By the time Confucianism was firmly established, during the Han and subsequent dynasties, it had become colored with Taoist and Buddhist teachings. As a result, in the Sung dynasty (960–1279 A.D.), it emerged as the *Li Hsüeh Chia* or School of Study of *Li*, which, in the West, is called Neo-Confucianism—a synthesis of Confucianism, Taoism and Buddhism. This is close to the form that has come down to the present day.

(7) During the Ch'ing (Manchu) dynasty an independent school of criticism arose that attacked the Neo-Confucianism of the preceding period. These critics, who continue to the present day, devoted themselves to linguistic studies and textual criticism at the expense of philosophical inquiry. On this account, they cannot be classified as a genuine school of philosophy.

(8) The dominant trend of thought in the New Culture Movement, which reached its climax in 1919, was toward Westernization, as expressed in positivism, pragmatism and materialism. This led to extensive questioning and criticism

of traditional institutions and outlooks from the viewpoints of utilitarianism and pragmatism.

(9) The Nationalist Movement of 1926 resulted in the establishment of the National Government, under the leadership of Chiang Kai-shek and the Kuomintang. The *Three People's Principle (San Min Chu I)* served as the basic text of the Nationalist Movement, and now the teachings of Confucius are advocated as the spiritual basis of the Nationalist resistance to Communism.

(10) The New Culture Movement of 1919 helped pave the way for Chinese Communism, which, strangely enough, has a good deal in common with Legalism. Both doctrines reject the appeal to tradition; both condemn Confucianism; both stand for authoritarian and totalitarian government. Thus, in the eyes of the Chinese, Communism is a revival of Legalism.

his contemporaries and to succeeding ages. He transformed feudal ceremonies into a system of ethics. His humanism contrasted sharply with the naturalism of Lao Tzŭ; he devoted his life to the ideal of an orderly society whose stress lay upon proper relations among civilized men.

The dominant position of Confucianism over the last twenty-five centuries is due only in part to the immortal Sage himself. He laid the foundations upon which Mencius and Hsün Tzŭ constructed a majestic temple where Chinese thought and culture have found fulfillment ever since. Mencius must be remembered as the great defender of Confucianism, who in an age of intellectual anarchy and heterodoxy defended the great tradition with such vigor and courage that it remained supreme. In addition, he expanded significantly on his master's teachings (Chapter 2).

While remaining loyal to Confucianism, Hsün Tzŭ

took a stand against Mencius—in particular against his doctrine of human nature. Mencius was an idealist in his dedicated faith in the goodness of human nature. Hsün Tzŭ placed little faith in human nature, with the result that he exalted the functions and prerogatives of the state. In this he anticipated the two great exponents of the third-century Legalist School, Han Fei Tzŭ and Li Ssŭ, who, although they were Legalists, remained essentially disciples of this great Confucian. Hsün Tzŭ is probably best placed as an eclectic; embodying the best intellectual achievements of the various schools of thought, he was able to summarize Confucius' doctrine for posterity (Chapter 7).

There was a third reaction to the period—that of Mo Tzŭ and his followers. Coming from a lower social class, Mo Tzŭ taught a philosophy of life corresponding to the desires of the common people and hence opposed the aristocratic leanings of both Confucius and Lao Tzŭ. Where they had both looked to the past—Lao Tzŭ, to undo civilization; Confucius, to sustain existing Chou culture—Mo Tzŭ took the utilitarian path of looking for happiness in a promising future that would be achieved by actively building a different and better world (Chapter 6).

In addition to these three great systems of philosophy, there were the Legalists, already mentioned, who made their influence felt in the third century B.C., during the transition from the Chou to the Ch'in period. Han Fei Tzŭ (died 233 B.C.) was the chief exponent of this school and a descendant of the royal house of the state of Han. His thought originated in existing doctrines—in the *shih* (authority) of Shên Tao, *shu* (statecraft) of Shên Pu-hai and *fa* (law) of Shang Yang. Han Fei Tzŭ also drew on Hsün Tzŭ's theory of human nature to support his contention that law was essential in keeping social order and peace. The Legalists, as typified by Han Fei Tzŭ, stood for firm and autocratic—even totalitarian—government and for stringent laws as the framework of social order. Thus, they came into conflict with Confucian scholars in particular and most past teachings in general, which stressed the dignity of the individual and the need for personal influence of the ruler.

This conflict was in a large measure responsible for the notorious edict of 213 B.C., issued by the Ch'in emperor Shih Huang Ti at the instigation of his Legalist minister, Li Ssŭ, ordering the destruction of the ancient classics, especially the books of the Confucian School. As a result of this edict, the intellectual activity of the previous period came to an abrupt end.

Such, in outline, are the four great systems of philosophy of the Chou period as represented by the eight great philosophers whose teachings and ideas have dominated the mind of China. Although they differ widely, these four schools have shaped the character of Chinese philosophy as a whole. The story of their development and meaning is the story of Chinese philosophy.

Confucius

我非生而知之者好古敏以求之者也

"I am not one born with possession of knowledge, but being fond of antiquity, I assiduously pursue it."
Analects, VII-19.

1. Confucius

Of all the great philosophers of China, Confucius is best known to the world. The name Confucius is the somewhat Latinized Western form of the Chinese K'ung Tzŭ, which literally means Master K'ung. Confucius was known first by his family name alone, the title Master having been added later as a sign of respect.

Confucius was the first to produce a great, all-embracing system of philosophy in China. Followed for twenty-five centuries, it has molded the habits and character of the Chinese people.

Before Confucius, China already possessed many treasures of literature and history, but they were scattered and apparently unrelated. What Confucius did was to assimilate all that was best in the ancient sages and kings; then, on the basis of this past heritage, to build a great system of philosophy. In his achievement, Confucius established himself as one of the greatest thinkers of all history.

[1]

THE LIFE OF CONFUCIUS

At fifteen, I set my mind on learning; at thirty, I stood firm to my purpose; at forty, I acted with discretion; at fifty, I knew Ming [Decree of Heaven]; at sixty, I comprehended truth; and now, at seventy, I can follow my heart's desire, without transgressing the sense of justice.*

Confucius' birth date is a matter of doubt, but that traditionally given, 551 B.C., cannot be far wrong. He was born in the state of Lu (modern Ch'u Fu, in Shantung), the cultural center of ancient China. Many events, dreams and portents have been associated with his birth. We are told, for instance, that Mother K'ung once prayed in a cave for a son, and the same night had a dream in which the Black Emperor (one of the Divine Beings) appeared and granted her request. When her time drew near, she ran to that same cave, where the child was born and "baptized" by a warm spring that gushed forth at the moment of birth. In the same story, it is said that Confucius, at birth, had a miraculous appearance, with a "wide mouth, ox lips and a dragon back." (The dragon, in China, is a symbol of royalty.) Although such myths are now recognized as imagi-

---

*All extracts in this chapter are from the *Analects*, unless otherwise noted.

nary, they serve well to show the esteem in which Confucius has been held by the Chinese.

Confucius came of a respectable family that could trace its origin to the ancient royal house of Shang. His ancestors had thus all been men of eminence in politics and letters. His father, the elder K'ung Shu Liang-heh, who was known as a soldier of daring, courage and prowess, died when Confucius was only three years old.

Not much is known of the Sage's boyhood under the care and instruction of his mother. He must have been a solemn child, for it is said that when he was six years old, he began to play with other children at "sage-kings," performing the ancient rites, arranging sacrificial vessels and assuming ceremonial postures. At the age of fifteen, he devoted himself to learning and gained a reputation for knowledge and propriety. Of knowledge Confucius later said:

> Men born with possession of knowledge are the highest type; those who gain it by study rank next; those who attain it only by hard study are the third; those who, although they study hard, do not attain it are the lowest.

As to his own case, he said that he was "not the one born with possession of knowledge," but being fond of study of the principles and institutions of antiquity, he assiduously pursued it.

Because of the death of his father, Confucius' family knew poverty, and he was at first unable to follow the path of pure scholarship. The young Confucius did receive the usual aristocratic education consisting of the arts of charioteering and archery, history and numbers, music and rituals; but he began his career as a granary overseer in his native district and had a successful term of office. The following year he was placed in charge of the public fields, and under his management, the cattle were strong and healthy. At a later period he told his pupils: "When I was young, my condition was low, and for this reason I acquired my ability in many things."

When he was nineteen years old, Confucius married a lady of the Chien-kwan family from the Sung state, and a son was born a year later. At the birth of the son, the Duke of Lu sent a pair of carp, the traditional symbol of domestic felicity and fertility. To commemorate the gift, Confucius named his son Li (the carp). Nothing is known of other children except that Confucius had at least one daughter.

In the year 528 B.C. Confucius abandoned his public employment to mourn the loss of his mother. During the three years' mourning, he refrained from sensual indulgences and activities and devoted himself to the study of ancient history, literature and institutions. We do not know what position he took after the period of mourning was over. Probably he commenced his career as a public teacher, for he had already commanded public attention and the respect of the great. For instance, in the year 518 B.C., while lying on his deathbed, Mêng Hsi-tzŭ, head of one of the three noble families in Lu, told his two sons to go and study the doctrines of antiquity under Confucius. It was through their influence that Confucius was later sent by Duke Chao of Lu to visit Lo, the imperial capital of Chou, for the purpose of observing the relics of lost imperial greatness.

Chou had long been politically inactive, but was still the center of culture. Although its glory had faded, traces of splendor were still discernible in its capital at Lo. Because Confucius went there not as a diplomat but as a visitor intent on studying the rites and music of the existing dynasty, he paid visits to the famous musician Ch'ang Hung and the curator of the royal archives, Lao Tan, better known to the entire world as Lao Tzŭ.

Ch'ang Hung, greatly impressed by the intellectual accomplishments of Confucius, made the following remarks:

When he speaks, he praises the ancient kings. He moves along the path of humility and courtesy. He has heard of every subject and has a good memory. His knowledge of things seems inexhaustible. Have we not in him the promise of a sage? [1]

But Lao Tzŭ reacted differently and gave Confucius a lesson on humility and the simple life:

All those men whom you talk about are dead, and their bones are moldered to dust; only their words remain. When the princely man has good

---
[1] Liu Wu-chi, *Confucius, His Life and Times*, p. 49.

fortune, he succeeds; but if circumstances are against him, then he proceeds as though his feet were entangled. I have heard that a good merchant having his treasures well stored looks as though he were destitute, and that the princely man being eminent in virtue appears as though he were stupid. Give up your proud airs and many desires; put away your artificial manners and sensual appetites. These are of no advantage to you. That is all I have to tell you. [2]

After the visit, Confucius, instead of being ruffled by this honest and blunt advice, said to his disciples:

I know birds can fly, fish can swim and animals can run. The runner may be snared; the swimmer may be hooked; the flier may be shot by the arrow. But as to dragons, I cannot tell how they mount on the wind and clouds high up in the air. Today, I have seen Lao Tzŭ. What a dragon! [3]

While we cannot prove the genuineness of this encounter, it may very well have taken place, since in Book XXIV of the *Li Chi* (*Book of Rites*) Confucius tells Chi K'ang what he once heard from Lao Tzŭ about ancient sage-kings, and in Book V he refers four times to views of Lao Tzŭ on certain points of funeral rites. It is interesting in any event that Confucius and Lao Tzŭ are represented as being immediately at

---

[2] *Shih Chi,* Vol. 63, Biog., Sec. III.
[3] *Ibid.*

odds. Over the ages, their respective philosophies have appeared similarly opposed: each great in its own right, but widely different from the other.

While at Lo, Confucius set off on many sight-seeing trips, which were to have great significance in his later thought and writings. He walked over the grounds set apart for the great sacrifices to Heaven and Earth, and he visited the Hall of the Grand Temple, where the ancestral rites of the sovereign were held. In the temple there was a metal statue of a man with three clasps upon his mouth, and on his back a homily which read: "Be careful of your speech. Don't talk too much, for talk leads to calamity." Confucius was struck by this and said to a disciple: "These words are true and commend themselves to our feelings."

Then Confucius was led to inspect the Hall of Light, built for the royal reception of visiting feudal princes. On the walls were painted portraits of ancient sovereigns, including those of Yao and Shun, King Wên and the Duke of Chou, who held the infant King Chêng on his knees. The dignity of the faces, the grandeur of the temple and the beauty of the hall, together with the greatness of the Duke, all impressed Confucius so profoundly that he turned to his companions, exclaiming: "Now I understand the wisdom of the Duke and see how the Chou house attained imperial eminence. As we use a mirror to reflect the forms of things, so we study antiquity to understand the present." [4]

---

[4] *Ibid.*

Although Confucius did not remain at Lo for long, the visit gave him a deeper understanding of his cultural inheritance and opened up new vistas for his further pursuit, while at the same time convincing him of the greatness of the Chou house.

Upon returning to Lu, Confucius continued his work of teaching. His fame greatly increased, and aspiring young men of all descriptions, eager to be instructed in the classics and in conduct and government, gathered to him.

Not until he was past fifty did Confucius enter into public life. At fifty-two, he was made Chief Magistrate of the town of Chung-tu and was soon promoted to the position of Minister of Justice. Later, when he had to give up his office in Lu, he spent thirteen or fourteen years abroad with a handful of students, traveling, teaching and visiting the feudal rulers of his time. When at last he was recalled to Lu, he was already an old man of sixty-eight, hardly able to make his influence felt in the government. Since his direct attempts had often been thwarted by official jealousy, he henceforth endeavored to attain his ends by less direct but more certain means. He devoted himself more than ever to the instruction of youth and to the editing and recording of ancient documents that formed the basis of his teaching.

In 482 B.C., he lost his only son; in 481 B.C., his favorite student, Yên Hui; and in 479 B.C., Confucius himself died at the age of seventy-three. He was buried at Chu-fu.

The career of the great Sage had been centered on three goals: to serve government; to teach youth; and to record Chinese culture for posterity. These three lines of activity, which were overlapping, will be discussed in the following sections.

[2]

CONFUCIUS AS A STATESMAN

Let the prince be as a prince; let the minister be as a minister. Let the father be as a father; let the son be as a son.

Confucius lived in the time when the central power of the Chou house was beginning to diminish so that the vassal states had their own ruling princes, each governing in his own way. Chinese historians call this age the Ch'un Ch'iu or Spring–Autumn period (722–481 B.C.). That which followed it is described as the Chan Kuo period or the period of the Warring States (480–222 B.C.), when the decay of central authority led to a total breakdown in the entire legal and social structure of the country and ceaseless wars. As the great advocate of order and dignity, Confucius preached against the growing chaos, stressing the responsibilities inherent in human relationships—between subject and state; even among members of a single family. Confucius had seen chaos arise in the world when the prince did not act as a prince or the minister as a minister and so on. Thus, he felt that the first step toward the transformation of a disordered world was to have everyone recognize and fulfill his own proper place.

Confucius' highest ideal was that of world government, which he called "Grand Commonwealth" (*Ta Tung*). His theory of this Grand Commonwealth is found in the *Li Yun* ("Evolution of Rites"), which is one of the chapters in the *Li Chi* (*Book of Rites*). The first stage of social progress is seen as a world of disorder; the second, as a world of "small tranquillity" or approaching peace in which all states enjoy order and peace; the third stage is that of the idyllic Grand Commonwealth, described as follows:

> When the great *Tao* [way] was practiced, a spirit of public welfare pervaded the world. Men of talent and virtue were chosen to positions of responsibility. Sincerity was emphasized and brotherhood cultivated. Therefore, men did not love only their own parents, nor did they treat as children only their own sons. The aged were cared for until death. There was employment for the able-bodied and means of sustenance for the young. Kindness and compassion were shown widows, orphans and those without children to care for them—and for those disabled by disease. Men had suitable work and women, their homes. They hated to see goods lying about in waste, yet they did not hoard them for their own use; they disliked the thought that their energies were not fully used, yet they used them not for their own benefit. Selfish schemings were repressed and not allowed to develop. Robbers, filchers and traitors no longer appeared, so that every man's front

door remained open without fear of harm of any kind. This was the age of the Grand Commonwealth.[5]

In mapping out a worldly career for himself, Confucius was inspired by the Duke of Chou. Thus, to achieve his lofty ideal of world government, Confucius first determined to wait for the appearance of an "enlightened sovereign," whom he would serve just as his revered Duke of Chou had served the Chou house.

If it was not his lot to give his great abilities to the service of an "enlightened sovereign," he would look for a serious-minded ruler who would invest him with high office and trust to his guidance, just as Duke Huan of the Ch'i state had entrusted himself to Kuan Chung, the famous statesman of the seventh century B.C. If even this were not possible, he would look forward to service in a small state to set an example of good government, just as Tzŭ Ch'an, the famous statesman of the sixth century B.C., did in the state of Chêng.

In any event, Confucius was not merely an idealist. Not only did he give a concrete picture of a kind of human society to aim for, but he also laid out a realistic program for his own life. Still further, when Tzŭ Kung, one of his favorite disciples, inquired about the essentials of good government, Confucius realistically outlined three things: abundance of food, adequate armaments and the confidence (*hsin*) of the people. Of the three, Confucius held the greatest to be the

---
[5] *Li Chi*, Bk. IV, Ch. 9

confidence of the people, without which "there would be no government." Elsewhere, Confucius said:

> The ruler of a state is not concerned about lack of wealth; he is concerned about fair distribution of wealth. He is not concerned about poverty, but about insecurity. When there is fair distribution, there will be no poverty; when there is harmony, there will be no complaint of shortage; when there is contentment, there will be no rebellion.

Social instability and economic inequality were the weaknesses of Lu, which Confucius tried to reform, but with little success. Although Duke Chao reigned over Lu, he was a mere puppet in the hands of three powerful families named Chi Sun, Shu Sun and Mêng Sun. The heads of the three families filled the three chief ministerial posts: those of instruction, works and war. In the year 517 B.C., when Confucius came back from the imperial capital, Duke Chao was driven from Lu by a domestic revolt and fled into Ch'i, the state adjoining Lu on the north.

As a gesture against the unruly events of the day, Confucius hastened to Ch'i in the wake of the ducal party. However, he did not join the Duke's retinue at the border town of Ch'i but went straight to its capital at Lin-tzŭ, some hundred miles north of Lu. His hope was to influence Ching, the reigning Duke of Ch'i, since Ch'i was the only nearby state capable of exercising any degree of influence on the affairs of Lu. However, although struck by the talents of the Sage,

Ching hesitated to take him into service, and Confucius returned to Lu.

Confucius had not made his trip to Ch'i entirely in vain since he was initiated for the first time into the beauties of Shao music, supposedly composed by the ancient sage-emperor Shun (2255?–2205 B.C.). He was so ravished by the exalting melodies that for three months he was oblivious to the taste of meat. "I never imagined," he asserted, "that music could have been made so excellent."

Confucius remained in Lu for a long period outside of government service because it was a time of such great disorder. After the death of the exiled Chao, the new Duke Ting also became a puppet of the three powerful clans. What was worse, even the great ministers themselves were now either being sent to prison or driven from their domains by Yang Hu, a powerful vassal of the Chi Sun clan, who was now virtually dictator of Lu. However, in the year 501 B.C., the chiefs of the three noble families, under the leadership of Mêng I Tzŭ, defeated Yang Hu and restored their positions in Lu. Because of his victorious campaign against Yang Hu, Mêng I Tzŭ, who had studied under Confucius, rose in the government, and it was largely through his influence that the Sage was made chief magistrate of Chêng-tu, an outlying town some twenty-eight miles west of the capital. Presently, Confucius was given the important post of Minister of Justice, next in rank only to the ministries of instruction, works and war, held by the chiefs of the three aristocratic families.

Although it was more than twenty years after the

death of Tzŭ Ch'an, the great statesman of Chêng, when Confucius held office in government, Tzŭ Ch'an's personality and achievements profoundly inspired Confucius in all the reforms he effected. He said:

> Tzŭ Ch'an possessed four virtues of Chun tzŭ [Superior Man]: [he was] courteous in his private conduct, punctilious in serving his superior, kind in his dealings with the people and just in exacting services from them.

Confucius was so successful in following his model and effected such improvement in the manners and morals of the people that Lu became the envy of all the neighboring states. Among other things, he stressed adequate nourishment of the populace. Different foods were prescribed for the old and the young, and tasks were assigned commensurate with strength. Men were then honest, and women, chaste; people even observed the custom of symbolizing their chastity by walking on opposite sides of the street. Valuables might be exposed on the road without risk of misappropriation; shepherds abandoned the practice of filling their sheep with water before leading them to market. Travelers from all parts of the empire felt at ease when they came to Lu.

Confucius' success here is further indication of how truly practical a man he was. A characteristic incident is recorded of his accompanying the Duke of Lu to an interview at Chia-ku with the powerful Duke of Ch'i, where it was proposed to settle old scores and possibly make an alliance. The chief officer to the Duke of Ch'i, dubbing Confucius a "man of ceremony without courage," advised his master to coerce the Duke of Lu with arms and annex a part of the border territory. But Confucius conducted the interview with such adroitness that he not only averted danger but also induced the discomfited Ch'i ruler to sign a treaty of alliance and restore the territory that he had unjustly appropriated from his rival.

This diplomatic triumph increased the popularity of Confucius and greatly strengthened his position. Soon after, he undertook an internal reform known as the "Destruction of Three Fortified Cities Campaign." The cities, Pi, Hou, and Chêng, held respectively by the clans of Ch'i, Shu Sun, and Mêng, were strongholds where domestic revolts often broke out. Hence, the objects of this campaign were twofold: first, to adopt precautions against domestic revolts by powerful vassals; and second, to check the growing power of the three clans. Confucius set himself energetically to the formidable task and succeeded in disarming Pi and Hou. The Mêng clan, however, still held to their city of Chêng; and its chief, a former student of Confucius, ignored the order for dismantling.

Under ordinary circumstances, Chêng would have offered no resistance. But just at the very moment when Confucius had put his own state on the right track, evil forces gathered to wreak vengeance on him. As a result of his internal reforms, Confucius had strengthened the ducal house and undermined the influence of the ministers. It thus became only a matter of time before Confucius would lose the confidence of the powerful families. If he should remain in government, he would certainly further centralize the ducal power and weaken theirs. Afraid of his reputation and jealous of his popularity, they increasingly regarded Confucius with distrust and aversion until they withdrew their support entirely.

At the same time, the Duke of Ch'i, after suffering the face-losing reverses of the Chia-ku conference, wanted to counteract the influence of the "man of ceremony" by forming a rift between him and his master. Resorting to the "stratagem of beauties," the Duke of Ch'i sent, instead of brave warriors or astute statesmen, eighty beautiful girls, skilled in dancing and singing and dressed in gaudy costumes, together with one hundred and twenty fine piebald horses. Being young and amorous, the Duke of Lu was caught in the snare and gave way to pleasure, abandoning all the lessons of propriety taught him by the Sage. For three mornings, he held no audience and neglected Confucius. Shortly after, Confucius embarked upon his wandering life.

One incident in particular made Confucius hasten away. There were three regular state services during the year—one in the spring and one at each of the solstices. At the spring feast, the Duke of Lu would provide sacrificial animals as a sign of gratitude to Heaven and Earth. As the time for this ceremony drew near, Confucius hoped that its magnitude and solemnity would put a limit to the Duke's frivolity. However, the ceremonies were rushed through, and the customary portion of the offerings was not sent to Confucius. Disappointed and disgusted, he could only hand in his resignation and leave Lu with a handful of students. This was in the year 497 B.C.

For the next fourteen years, Confucius wandered from state to state in search of patronage and the opportunity for working out his ideal of government. Although details of these travels are few, it is known that he first went to Wei, a then populous state with great possibilities of development and growth. He at once perceived its need for greater wealth and then for education. And he vowed to his disciples:

> Should I be invested with office, I would attain some improvement within one year and complete success within three years.

But the Duke of Wei at that time was preoccupied with the beauty and wit of a brilliant concubine, and a man of austere virtue such as Confucius was hardly to his taste. Hence, the court of Wei was clearly no place for him, and Confucius soon left for other states.

Not much is known of his wandering life after that, but it cannot be far wrong to say that he visited Sung, Chên and Ch'u. After several years in Chên, he returned to Wei in 483 B.C., and in the same year, when he was about sixty-eight years old, he was recalled to Lu. As he traveled, he met nothing but rebuff and disappointment, with none of the rulers willing to listen to him. At various times, he even endured physical danger and hardship. While in Sung, Confucius and his disciples narrowly escaped death from an armed band sent by Huan T'ui, the minister of Sung. Once, the people of Kuang mistook Confucius for his old enemy, the powerful Yang Hu, and besieged him. Only Confucius' patience and dignity restrained tempers until he was recognized. At another time, when in an outlying area, he and his band ran out of provisions and barely missed starvation. A vivid indication of Confucius' courage and determination can be had from his comment when faced with this situation:

> A gentleman stands firm in his misery. It is the small man who gives way to license in times of trouble.

Confucius was true to his preaching and always bore hardships with splendid heroism and little complaining. When not in actual physical difficulty, he was often exposed to criticism and ridicule, especially at the hands of Taoists.

About this time, Confucius and his followers encountered two recluses, men who had withdrawn from the world in disgust at the waywardness of the times. One of them said to Tzŭ Lu, a disciple of the Sage:

> The whole world is in turmoil like a swelling flood, and what man is he to change it? You are now following one who merely withdraws from this man and that. Would it not be better for you to follow those who withdraw from the world altogether?

When Tzŭ Lu reported this, Confucius gave the wisest possible answer:

We cannot associate with birds and beasts. If not with our fellow men, with whom should I associate?

On a similar occasion, Tzŭ Lu spoke out directly for his master in words that aptly sum up Confucius' reasons for his persistent, if frustrating, travels:

To refuse to serve in the government is not right. Since the relationship between the old and the young must be maintained, how can the relationship between the ruler and the ruled be abolished? Wishing to maintain one's own personal purity, one neglects the great relations of mankind. The superior man serves in the government because it is his duty to do so. The fact that he is bound to fail, he knows already.

One final passage from the *Analects* should be noted:

When Tzŭ Lu arrived to pass the night in the city of Shi-mên, the gatekeeper asked: "Where are you coming from?"
"From Confucius."
"Is he not the man who is undertaking something even though he knows what he does is in vain?"

The last sentence is a concrete picture of Confucius.

[3]

CONFUCIUS AS AN EDUCATOR

There is no distinction of class in education.

Confucius' great ambition lay in politics, but his great achievement was in education. He was an educator of great skill and reputation, with a group of aspiring young men of all descriptions ever at his side. Bearing as little as a bundle of dried meat for tuition, they came to be instructed in the knowledge of *li* (rites) and accompanying arts. This form of education was a great innovation of the Chou world. Prior to that time, all branches of learning had been in the official custody of hereditary aristocrats, with no such thing as a private individual engaged in teaching the great mass of the common people. Confucius was thus the first teacher in China to make education available to all. He asserted:

> I have never refused instruction to anyone eager for learning, even if but a bundle of dried meat be offered me.

He qualified this only in that he would not instruct anyone not eager to learn; nor would he teach those incapable of forming their own ideas. He continued:

> Nor would I give further teaching to one who,

after I have made clear one corner of the subject, cannot deduce the other three.

The greatness of Confucius is attested to by the fact that since his time education has always had a place for talented youths who might rise by their study and effort from lowly origins to higher ranks.

When he retired into private life, Confucius had attracted young men of promise from all parts of China, among whom were many eminent in virtue, in letters and in politics. When he was recalled to his native state, he persuaded the Duke of Lu to take some of these students into his service. Though it is probably an exaggeration, it is said that no fewer than three thousand received his instruction. However, the names of only seventy-two can definitely be ascertained, and twenty-five are enrolled on the national historical records.

The students who accompanied him in his wanderings and enjoyed his personal teachings were divided into four groups: first, those men noted for their virtues; second, those gifted in the art of speech; third, those distinguished in government; and fourth, those eminent in literature. Many of these senior students later became accomplished scholars and thinkers in their own right. It was largely through them that Confucius exerted a great influence in the development of Chinese culture and won for himself the title of "Su Wang" or the "Unsceptered Monarch," whose intellectual sway has been acknowledged by the ages.

Generally speaking, the education offered by Confucius was one in ethics and in the arts. Among the latter, rites, music and poetry were fundamental. According to Confucius, rites, as an institution, regulate our mind and direct our desires. Music, as a "civilizing force," harmonizes our sentiments and restrains our passions. Poetry, as a "moral force," moderates our nature and inspires our ethical feeling. Thus, the arts are important of themselves, but they are also the foundation of ethical learning. In Confucius' words:

> [Our character] is cultivated by poetry, established by rites and perfected by music.

In addition to poetry, rites and music, *Shu* (History), *Yi* (Change), and *Ch'un Ch'iu* (Spring and Autumn) were also taught. Together, these are the so-called Six Classics, which constituted the cultural legacy of the past and later became a common term for the content of the classical education. In the Taoist *Chuang Tzŭ* (Chapter XXXIII, *Tien Hsia*), the specific purpose of each of these subjects is given:

> Poetry is to teach ideals; History is to teach events; Rites is to teach conduct; Music is to teach harmony; Change is to teach the dual forces of the universe; and Spring and Autumn is to teach the great principle of honor and duty.

As in the practical application of the arts already noted above, the stress here is on the use of education in the development of personality rather than upon knowledge for its own sake.

With regard to the learning process, Confucius said:

> Study without thought is in vain; thought without study is dangerous.

He further maintained that, above all, a man should have a clear and realistic view of his own limitations. He once said to Tzǔ Lu:

> Let me teach the way to knowledge. Only say that you know when you really know, and concede your ignorance of what you do not know. This is the way to knowledge.

The basic factor underlying Confucius' zeal for educating all men was his conviction that men are largely alike at birth only to be set apart by the habits and idiosyncrasies they acquire, i.e., by knowledge. Confucius' concern was to ensure that acquired knowledge would lead man to select that which is good. Thus, Confucius viewed his own function as an educator as an ethical and moral one. His purpose was to educate so that men would choose good and by doing this improve their own lot and that of mankind as a whole.

Finally, of himself, Confucius said:

> There are people who act without knowing why. But I am not like those. I hear much and then select the good and follow it. I see much and then

learn and memorize it. This comes next to true knowledge.

And again, he characterized himself as a teacher whose function was

> ... to take notes of things in silence, to treasure up knowledge despite much study and never to weary of teaching others.

These were the characteristics of the greatest teacher in the history of China. It is only natural that his birthday has been designated "National Teachers' Day."

[4]

CONFUCIUS AS A PHILOSOPHER

There is one central idea that runs through my thought.

Amid the mass of knowledge that Confucius developed, the central idea of the whole system is the doctrine of *jen* or "human-heartedness." All else is but deduction from this: his ethics, his politics, his life ideals—all flow from this governing doctrine.

Jen expresses the Confucian ideal of cultivating humanity, developing human faculties, sublimating one's personality and upholding human rights. Chu Hsi (1130–1200 A.D.), a famous Confucian scholar of the Sung Dynasty, defined *jen* as "the virtue of the soul," "the principle of love" and "the center of Heaven and Earth." The ideograph for *jen* is composed of two characters, "man" and "two," showing the stress not on man alone but in relation to his fellow men. Confucius held that human relations should be based on the moral sentiment of *jen*, which leads to positive efforts for the good of others. He said: *"Jen consists in loving others."* In fact, Confucius regarded *jen* not merely as a special kind of virtue but as all the virtues combined. Hence, it may be defined as "perfect virtue."

The idea of *jen* may be expressed in the conceptions of *hsiao* or filial piety and *ti* or fraternal love. These two concepts express the same unselfish human feeling —filial piety signifying a state of spiritual communion in the eternity of time, and fraternal love signifying a state of spiritual communion in the infinity of space.

> A youth when at home should practice filial piety; when abroad, fraternal love. He should be earnest and sincere, loving to all, and fond of *jen*.

Confucius, with his keen sense of practicality, made the virtues of filial piety and fraternal love the cornerstones of the social structure. By extending them in time and in space, and diffusing their influence through all other related virtues, he made them both the bond of social solidarity and the connection between succeeding generations. In their broader extensions, filial piety and fraternal love become the rational basis for the love due to men.

In the *Analects*, two other similar concepts are introduced; namely, *chung* or faithfulness and *shu* or altruism. The former means the state of mind when one is completely honest with oneself, while the latter is the state of mind when one is in complete understanding and sympathy with the outside world. The Chinese character for *chung* is made up of the components "middle" and "heart." With one's heart in the very center, one will be faithful to one's self by being sympathetic to others. In Confucius' words:

> The man of *jen* is one who, wishing to sustain himself, sustains others, and wishing to develop himself, develops others.

Chung is the positive way to practice *jen*.

The Chinese word *shu* has the meaning of "as one's heart"; that is, to do to others as your heart prompts you. As to the significance of *shu*, Confucius said:

> Do not do to others what you do not wish yourself.

This is the negative way to practice *jen*. The concepts of *chung* and *shu* are the same as those of *hsiao* and *ti*, only the latter refer principally to the relations within the family, while the former have a wider, less specific import. In both cases, the concern is for a state of mind where true and unselfish love is dominant.

The principle of *jen* has become a mighty factor in the continuity and perpetuity of Chinese culture and national existence. It has never encountered any system of ideas that could withstand its influence. Its lesson of justice and fairness, of a spirit of tolerance and of mutual affection, is as pertinent today as ever—not only for China but the world as a whole.

[5]

CONFUCIUS AND THE SIX CLASSICS

I transmit, but I do not create; I have faith in and love for ancient studies.

Although it remains a matter of controversy, it is now most commonly accepted that the above modest account is more or less accurate, that the great body of knowledge known as the Six Classics existed before Confucius' time, but that these works were preserved and transmitted to posterity largely through Confucius' labors. Confucius started out by studying the ancient materials in the hope of putting them into practice in actual government. It was only late in life that he turned to edit and record them for the benefit of future generations. And it was while he was performing this task that he gave the ancient institutions new interpretations derived from his own ethical concepts.

Obviously, some acquaintance with the Six Classics is essential for an appreciation of Confucius' achievement:

1. *Shu Ching* or the *Book of History:* The historical records collected and edited by Confucius contained 100 documents of early dynasties and covered a period extending from the twenty-fourth to the eighth century

28 / *The Story of Chinese Philosophy*

B.C. Confucius arranged these documents chronologically and wrote prefaces to them. The greater part of these materials was found in the archives of the Chou dynasty and consisted of dialogues on questions of state between emperors and their ministers, outlines of national policy, morale-building oaths taken before going to war, edicts and ordinances and records of ceremonial occasions. A minor part of the documents consisted of recollections of stories and sayings concerning the great men of early dynasties. All these documents were permeated with religious ideas and didactic passages.

Confucius compiled and arranged the documents for the purpose of making students "become conversant with facts" concerning the causes of the rise and fall of dynasties. Of the 100 documents he edited, only 28 are extant in the current *Book of History*. They are the best historical materials in existence for the study of ancient Chinese history and political thought.

2. *Shih Ching* or the *Book of Poetry:* The *Book of Poetry* is a collection of popular poems, written during the 500 years between the beginning of the Chou dynasty (twelfth century B.C.) and the period of Spring and Autumn (eighth to fifth centuries B.C.). Confucius selected 305 poems out of more than 3,000 pieces and arranged them under four heads: first, poems about the relationship between the sexes; second, "minor orthodox poems" for ordinary festivities; third, "major orthodox poems" for state festivities; and fourth, sacrificial poems for temple dances and entertainment. These pieces comprised the basic instruction Confucius offered his students in poetry.

His reasons for teaching poetry were several. During the Spring and Autumn period, it was customary in polite society to illustrate conversation with verses. Thus, Confucius was led to remark:

> Without studying the poems, one will have no hold on words.

Apart from this rhetorical function, however, Confucius stressed the moral value of the poems and summed up the benefits of studying them as follows:

> Poetry evokes inspiration and leads to introspection; it contributes to one's sociability and liberates one's frustration. In the study of poetry, one learns to serve one's parents and prince; besides, one is better acquainted with the names of birds and beasts, weeds and trees.

3. *Yao* or the *Music:* In Confucius' time, music was closely related to poetry. Thus, when he edited the collection of ancient poems, he arranged a musical setting for each of those he finally selected, either revising the old tunes or composing new ones. That is all we now know of Confucius' achievement here since none of this music has been preserved. We do know that there were four kinds of music, just as there were four types of poetry: Shao music, Chou, orthodox and temple music. That Confucius had an intimate knowledge of music and that he may even have been a musician, we learn from passages such as the following

where he spoke quite professionally to the Grand Music Master of Lu:

> The basic principle of music seems to be this: in beginning to play a piece, all the parts should sound grandiloquently together. As it gains momentum, the rhythm should be distinct and the notes clear. Then the piece should be played to completion in harmony without any jarring break.

As we might expect, Confucius attached the utmost importance to the moral effect of music and believed that it not only could "harmonize one's sentiment" but also "bring order out of the social chaos." In order to strengthen its moral effect, Confucius advanced the opinion that music should be popularized within limitations set by the state. For example, he proposed to censor Chêng music on the grounds that it was indecent and undesirable.

The satisfaction he gained from his work in music is hinted at in the following passage from the *Analects:*

> Only after my return to Lu from Wei did I begin to set music on its right track. Orthodox music and temple music were all set in their proper order.

4. *Li Chi* or the *Book of Rites:* "Without studying rites, one will not be able to establish oneself." In early times, rites were limited to religious observances, but they later came to govern all kinds of secular oc-

casions as well—including events such as archery contests and meetings of feudal princes. Hence, *li* may be defined as the mode or format of social practice in ancient China.

Long before Confucius' time there already existed an unwritten code known as *li*, but the great Duke of Chou was first to define, fix and set it down in writing. There must have been many discrepancies between this written version and the unwritten ones of past ages—just as there must have been differences among the traditional *li* of the various feudal states, some of which, as a result of ignorance, ended up with practices contrary to the true spirit of *li*.

From references in his works, we learn that Confucius edited a book dealing with rites to correct this undesirable situation. Although Confucius was versed in the rites, not only of Chou, but also of the two earlier dynasties of Hsia and Shang, it was the more "complete and elegant" ceremony of Chou that appealed to him. This is not surprising since he was a conservative in all his ideas about *li*. He stressed the origin and significance of the ancient ceremonies, and he recalled that *li* was an expression of sentiment. He criticized the debased practices of the time, terming *li* without sentiment as nothing more than mock ceremony. He asked indignantly:

> When one refers to rites, does one mean merely the offerings of jade and silk?

On another occasion, he said:

. . . as for mourning rites, there should be deep grief rather than minute attention to details.

5. *Yi Ching* or the *Book of Changes:* Of all the ancient books that Confucius studied, the *Yi Ching* or *Book of Changes* was his favorite. He used it so much that he wore out the strings of the binding on his copy three times. This book contains a fanciful system of philosophy, based on Eight Trigrams, consisting of triplet combinations or arrangements of a solid line and a divided line, either one of which necessarily appears twice, so as to make up the triplet. These Eight Trigrams are said to have been suggested in the reign of Fu Hsi (2852 B.C.?) by the mysterious markings on the shell of a tortoise. Interpretations were given to the trigrams by King Wên of Chou and his son, the Duke of Chou. Prior to Confucius, the book was used for divination. By means of the trigrams, the Chinese grasped at the mysteries of the universe and tried to show people how to avoid misfortune and to take advantage of opportunities. Like the *Book of Poetry*, this book is characteristic of the genius of the ancient Chinese in that it couples the aesthetic and the practical, the primitively simple with artistic symbols revealing depths of knowledge. It is at the same time a book of philosophy and a work of art—a combination of the abstract and concrete.

According to the *Book of Changes*, the universe is composed of *yin* and *yang*. The solid line represents *yang;* the broken one, *yin*. These are the dual forces of nature. *Yang* is the Male and *yin* the Female. They are, then, Heaven and Earth, Sun and Moon,

Light and Darkness, Life and Death. Obviously, these two basic symbols were limited and too simple for extended use, so in time the ancient sages hit upon the idea of putting three lines together to form a trigram. The result was the first Eight Trigrams, symbolizing natural phenomena: Heaven (☰), Earth (☷), Thunder (☳), Water (☵), Mountain (☶), Wind (☴), Fire (☲) and Marshes (☱).

These original Eight Trigrams did not receive philosophical significance, however, until Confucius added to them the Ten Wings or appendixes, and subsequently expanded the Eight Trigrams to Sixty-four Hexagrams. Each hexagram was supposed to be a symbolic representation of one or more phenomena of the universe, either natural or human. For example, the hexagram *ye* (☴☳) is formed by combining the trigram meaning wind, wood and penetration (☴) and the trigram meaning thunder, motion, and growth (☳). Hence, the hexagram *ye* represents the symbol of penetration of wood from above and growth below.

6. *Ch'un Ch'iu* or the *Spring and Autumn Annals:* Prolific as an editor, Confucius seems to have authored little; the *Ch'un Ch'iu* or *Spring and Autumn Annals* is generally regarded as his only work. It is a chronological record of the chief events in the state of Lu from the first year of Duke Yin's rule (722 B.C.) to the fourteenth of Duke Ai's (481 B.C.). The *Annals* owe their name to the tradition of prefixing each entry with the year, month, day and season when the event took place. Since spring then included summer,

and autumn, winter, the entries are all preceded by one of these two terms, with a resulting profusion of "spring" and "autumn."

The book is like a diary in which all events, great and small, are strung like beads on a string of days. The entries are all as brief as possible, covering every conceivable type of human affair and natural phenomenon. While this is a good way to collect materials, it is hardly sufficient to produce what could be classified as history. However, the greatness of this book lies not in its being a model history but in its other characteristics: First, Confucius departed from tradition when, although basing his materials on the official records of Lu, he rejected a narrow nationalistic attitude and stressed interstate organization and overall peace and unity. Secondly, in this book Confucius taught the divine duty of loyalty, generally spoken of as *Ch'un Ch'iu Tai Yi* or the "Great Principle of Honor and Duty of the Spring and Autumn." All the evils and vices and dissolutions of those days Confucius recorded without gloss, and he was just as unsparing in his conclusions of praise or blame. It is these judgments that reveal his philosophy of history, which, as we might expect, was a didactic one. The central theme of the *Annals* is to set up the norms of good government, to put usurping princes back in their proper places and to condemn misbehaving ministers, so that the cause of world peace and unity might be upheld. Thirdly, where the recording of history had traditionally been an official function, Confucius made it popular, and he made history a branch of study for common people. In addition, because of its mass of facts, the *Spring and Autumn Annals* is a grammar of Chinese politics.

[6]

AN ESTIMATE

The great mountain crumbles—
The strong beam breaks—
And the sage withers away.[6]

These were the words that Confucius murmured over and over early one morning, upon awakening from a dream that portended his death. He went on to say:

Since no enlightened king has arisen, there is no one under Heaven who will take me as his master. My end, I fear, is near.

Confucius stayed in bed, and died seven days later—in the fourth month of the year 479 B.C., when he was seventy-three.

He was buried near his native town, and many of his disciples stayed there for three years mourning for him. Even after the lapse of twenty-five centuries, in nearly every city Confucius had a temple, where his followers visited at every festival and per-

---
[6] *Shih Chi*, Vol. 47, Sec. 17.

formed the rites that he had taught. In all these temples, there was a central inscription that read: "He forms a triad with Heaven and Earth," i.e., in the person of Confucius the dual powers of Heaven and Earth had found their harmony perfected and made complete. This statement indicates something of the reverence in which Confucius had been held by the multitude of Chinese people.

The dominant position held by Confucius in China's intellectual life continued unchallenged for almost twenty-five centuries. His doctrine was long ago accepted as state teaching; his works were elevated as classics to be studied in schools; and his moral virtues regarded as the norms of society. As a matter of fact, the Chinese are essentially Confucian in their outlook and mentality; and except for the Buddhist and Taoist trends in the arts and letters, Chinese culture and Confucianism are almost synonymous, if not completely so.

However, since things have changed rapidly in modern China, it is worthwhile to re-examine the traditional and historical attitude toward Confucius and his teachings. The best starting point for such consideration is the doctrine of *jen*.

As we have seen, *jen* emphasizes human relations; it teaches one to be a good ruler, a good citizen, a good parent, a good child, a good husband, a good wife and a good neighbor; it advocates filial devotion and fraternity, justice and fairness, kindness and mutual affection. All these are the norms of Chinese conduct and keep people as brothers in the world. As such, *jen* has been a mighty factor in the continuity and perpetuity of Chinese culture. If modern civilization is to survive, human relations, instead of being based on domination and exploitation, must be founded on the great principle of *jen*.

However, Confucius' system has its defects. In the first place, it is too exclusively humanistic. It teaches how to deal with human affairs, but not how to control physical environment. It attempts to know *ming* (fate), but not to overcome it. It purports to secure the mean and be moderate, but not to go to the extreme and be aggressive. Confucius expressed this when he said:

> Living on coarse rice, simple vegetables and plain water, with bent arm on pillow, I am still happy. Ill-gotten wealth and honors are to me as wandering clouds.

And again:

> I murmur not against Heaven, nor complain against man. Learning from the lowest, I have come to know what is noble and lofty. Only does Heaven know me.

Unfortunately, while advancing individual fortitude, this ideal of life has no perceptible effect on promoting economic or social improvement. It neglects the progress of world civilization and largely overlooks the evolving material needs of man. It is a static rather than a dynamic influence; it is negative rather than positive. It makes for exertion and strain, but not for progress, because the means of progress are invention and discovery, for which Confucius failed to lay the foundation.

Another major defect lies in its veneration of the past. Confucius' system was built on the foundation of antiquity and emphasized this at the expense of adjusting to changing conditions of civilization. In the habit of searching the past, his philosophy succeeded in contributing to continuity and stability but interfered with new ideas and the forces of progress. As a traditionalist, Confucius felt that if each man followed tradition, society would of itself be perfect. Thus, the old systems are to be preserved but not reformed; the ideas of the past are to be venerated but not criticized. The result has been an overbalanced conservatism that the modern revolutionary Chinese are most emphatic in condemning.

A final defect is Confucius' failure to recognize in his scheme of government the worth and importance of the common people. While he emphasized harmonious relations between ruler and ruled and while he made education a democratic process, Confucius still seemed to place too much stress on the ruler—to the disadvantage of the ruled.

> The prince is the wind; the common people, the grass; and the grass bends in the direction of the wind.

The same note is struck in his three fundamental principles of ideal government:

First, if right principle prevailed through the world, rites and music and punitive wars would be originated by the Emperor. Second, if right principle prevailed through the world, the powers of government would not be in the hands of the ministers. Third, if right principle prevailed through the world, the common people would not criticize the government.

Confucius understandably worked for government under a king or emperor because he was disgusted with the wars of feudal lords and aristocratic families. A world of strong centralized governments appealed to him as an inevitably stable one. But, in fact, these political ideas, necessary at first for social stability, later suffered much in the hands of politicians and emperors who used Confucius' great authority and standing to justify their autocratic rule.

In spite of these defects, the philosophy of Confucius is one of the greatest the world has seen. Certainly, his grand conception of *jen*, the acme of the man-to-man relationship, is a great contribution to political philosophy, as well as to ethics. Moreover, although we deny the belief that Confucius could be anything like a savior of the modern world, his role as an inspiring and indefatigable teacher must remain high in history and his works in the rank of the great classics.

Mencius

"Treat the aged in your family as they should be treated and extend this treatment to the aged of other people's families. Treat the young in your family as they should be treated and extend this treatment to the young of other people's families."
Mêng Tzŭ, I, i, VII.

2. Mencius

Before the end of the Chou dynasty, several schools of thought developed within the Confucian tradition. But until the appearance of Mencius, there was no man of superior caliber to guarantee the triumph of Confucianism. With his winning eloquence, moral courage and deep conviction, Mencius popularized the teachings of Confucius, at the same time zealously attacking the heterodox teachings of other schools. In his contributions to Confucianism, as well as in his defense of the great tradition, Mencius has been generally recognized as the greatest philosopher after Confucius, "the Second Sage."

[1]

LIFE AND WRITINGS

Mencius (Mêng K'o) is the Latinized form of the name Mêng Tzŭ (Master Mêng). He was born a little over a hundred years after the death of Confucius, his approximate dates being 372–289 B.C. Like Confucius, Mencius had many legends associated with his birth. An angel supposedly appeared to his mother; and at the moment of birth, a brilliant, multicolored light is said to have illuminated the entire area. As is true with the Sage, such tales are more correctly an index of faith and of reverence than of fact.

Mencius was a native of the state of Tsou (the modern district of Tsou Hsien, in Shantung province) and it is said that he came of the aristocratic Mêng Sun family of Lu. When the old houses had started to collapse, the Mêng family had left Lu for shelter in Tsou. Like Confucius, Mencius lost his father early in life, being only three years old when he died. He was then brought up under the devoted care and instruction of Mother Mêng, whose name is a household word even to this day.

The favorite story about Mother Mêng concerns her moving three times in quest of a favorable environment for her son's upbringing. They lived near a cemetery until the mother discovered her son's favorite game was that of playing at burying and mourning the dead. They moved at once, near a market place, where the boy was soon playing at buying and selling. This, too, displeased the mother, so they moved again, this time to the vicinity of a school. Here, the sensitive child was free to pattern his actions after those of pupils and teachers—and the mother was happy. This story, and many like it, have served to inspire countless Chinese mothers ever since.

Early in life, Mencius came to regard Confucius as his greatest inspiration. He once said:

From the time that human life appeared on earth

down to this day, there never has been another
Confucius. . . . What I wish to do is to learn to
be like him. . . . Although I could not be a
disciple of Confucius himself, I have endeavored
to cultivate my virtue by means of others who
were.*

However, the two sages were entirely different in
temperament. Confucius had been an introvert and
a refined gentleman, cautious and deliberate in
speech; Mencius was an extrovert and a great oracle
of his age, widely noted for his wit. When asked a
difficult question or when under verbal attack, Confucius had often become helpless, and he had called
on Heaven to be his witness. Not so Mencius—he
characteristically lashed out at his opponents and
drove them into defensive positions.

Most of his working life appears to have been in
the second half of the fourth century B.C., when the
old China was beginning to disappear and great
changes were in progress. As we shall see in the next
section, this period was one of social disturbance,
political instability and intellectual anarchy, with the
result that Mencius' attempts at political influence
met with no greater success than had those of his
model. In the *Historical Records* (*Shih Chi*) of Ssŭ-
ma Ch'ien, we read:

Having achieved full comprehension of Confucian

---

*All extracts in this chapter are from the *Mêng Tzŭ* of Mencius, unless otherwise noted.

doctrine, he was taken into the service of King
Hsüan of Ch'i, but the king would not carry out
his principles. Thence, he went to Liang state,
but King Hui did not listen to his advice. To the
sovereigns, his words were like prayers of sorcery
and had no basis in fact.[1]

Contrary to the chronology given in this quotation,
it is now believed that Mencius' stay at Liang preceded that at Ch'i—that he arrived in the former in
320 B.C., subsequently departing for Ch'i in 318 B.C.

The records of his stay in Liang reveal the inevitable difficulties he encountered, inevitable because his meetings with feudal lords were really a
clash between the spiritual and physical worlds. In
that time of upheaval, King Hui of Liang sought to
strengthen his weak holdings by surrounding himself
with the best talents available. Being interested in
government, Mencius went to the court of Liang,
where his reputation earned him an immediate welcome. However, as soon as King Hui asked him for
advice on how to profit the kingdom, it became apparent that Mencius would be of little use in the
struggle for power. Ideas of profit were alien to
Mencius, and he replied:

> Why must Your Majesty speak of profit? It
> suffices if the principles of human-heartedness
> and righteousness prevail.

---
[1] *Shih Chi*, LXVL, Biog., Sec. 14.

He then argued that if the king were interested only in profit for his country, the great ministers in profit for their families, the petty officials and the common people in profit for their persons, then superiors and inferiors would fight one another for gains, and the kingdom would be in great danger.

> For if the people consider profit more important than righteousness, they will not be satisfied without depriving others of their possessions. There has never been a man trained in human-heartedness who neglected his parents, nor has there been a man trained in righteousness who overlooked his sovereign. Let Your Majesty speak of human-heartedness and righteousness and of nothing else. Why must you speak of profit?

On another occasion, King Hui complained that he had suffered military defeat, disgrace, loss of territory and even the death of his eldest son. He asked Mencius what course of action he should pursue to avenge himself. Mencius' reply was hardly welcome to the harassed king: He advised him not to rely on brute force, rather to carry out good government by diminishing punishments, abolishing exorbitant taxes and cultivating his own personal virtues. Mencius continued:

> Under conditions such as these, your people could be employed with wooden staffs to oppose the strong mail and sharp weapons of [enemy] troops.

Obviously, Mencius' words fell on deaf ears, and he found himself with little opportunity for exercising his influence in government. In a period of peace, he could well have hoped for success, but the expediency required by the times doomed his efforts. Mencius stayed in Liang until the end of the year 319 B.C., when King Hui died and was succeeded by his son, King Hsiang. After his first interview with the young king, Mencius said:

> When I looked at him from a distance, he did not appear like a sovereign. When I drew near to him, I felt no reverence for him.

In fact, Mencius was so disgusted that he soon left for Ch'i.

Ch'i had been dormant for about two centuries, but under the reign of King Hsüan it rose once more to prominence. He opened his doors to all men of talent with a thirst for politics, and many notable intellectuals and scholar-diplomats flocked into his court. He lodged them in magnificent quarters and gave them rich emoluments and honorary titles— everything except positions in government. This was so they could be free for their sole duty, that of advising him on government and discoursing on their learning.

When King Hsüan heard that Mencius was coming to Ch'i, he sent his son to meet him at the border, and when he offered him a high post at court, it seemed that Ch'i was the promising market where Mencius could finally sell his wares. However, the old difficulties were present since, after all, King Hsüan was like other feudal lords in his concern for increased military strength that might gain the imperial throne and in his self-confessed weaknesses for beauty and wealth. Well versed in polite literature and learned discourse, Mencius did try to adapt himself to the king's disposition. He suggested that imperial sway might yet be possible, in spite of the king's weaknesses, provided that he would consent to share his pleasures with the people. But, in the end, Mencius could not resist being his true self, and as in the following dialogue, his bluntness served only to isolate him. Mencius asked the king:

"Suppose your minister were to entrust his wife and children to a friend while he went on a journey and that, on his return, discovered that his wife and children had been cold and hungry. What should he do to his friend?"

"Cast him off!" replied the king.

"Suppose that your Chief Magistrate could not regulate his officers. How would you deal with him?"

"Dismiss him!" came the ready answer.

"Suppose, then, that within your kingdom, there is no good government. What should be done?"

The king turned his head and spoke of other matters.

The king was ever courteous and often lent Mencius a friendly ear, but he was never interested enough to try the theory of good government. In time, Mencius realized that the attentive and respectful audiences he received were only that, and nonproductive—so he left Ch'i.

Like Confucius, Mencius was never completely disappointed, although he finally had to concede the futility of his efforts. He was sixty-one years old when he left Ch'i in 312 B.C. to continue his search for an enlightened prince. He did have one further opportunity at a court—in T'êng, a small principality between the two powerful states of Ch'u and Ch'i. Duke Wên of T'êng was having difficulty in fending off his aggressive neighbors, and he requested Mencius' help. Mencius declined the high post offered him when he saw that it was of doubtful sincerity, but he did advise the duke on many things, mainly on a land-reform system known as the *ching-t'ien,* or "well-field" system (*see page* 63). But his stay was brief, and in 307 B.C. he went to Lu and retired into private life, devoting himself to the instruction of youth and to the preparation of his philosophical record, known as *Mêng Tzŭ.* Like Confucius, Mencius was a highly successful educator, loved by his disciples. His *Mêng Tzŭ* ranks as one of the greatest books of the Confucian school. In 289 B.C., at the age of eighty-four, Mencius died in his native state.

[2]

MENCIUS AND HIS TIME

Some additional comment is necessary about the age that Mencius lived in, appropriately known by historians as the era of *Ch'un Kuo* or "Warring States." As we have seen, it was a time of chaos when the central government of the Chou house finally lost control, and a struggle for power among the various feudal states ensued. The Age of Warring States can be characterized in the following terms:

First, war was the chief feature of this time—on several levels. On the one hand, the great states (basically seven in number) fought for the prestige and power inherent in the imperial throne. On the other hand, and growing out of this situation, the lesser, weaker states were forced into a posture of self-defense and a struggle for survival. Duke Wên of T'êng, complaining to Mencius for advice, summarized this situation:

> T'êng is a small state. Though I do my utmost to serve those large states, yet we cannot escape suffering from them. What course shall I take that we may do so?

Second, wars brought with them, not only the burden of military service, but, inevitably, high taxes. The result for the people was miserable poverty in years of good harvest, starvation and death in years of famine.

Third, this was the age of the wandering diplomats and politicians, really nothing more than a breed of high-level opportunistic mercenaries. King Hui of Liang was not alone in surrounding himself with the best available minds. In their urgency for success, nearly all the insecure feudal rulers seized talent where they found it—the talent, in turn, grasping every opportunity for power in their own personal behalf. Often, the princes became pawns in the skillful hands of their aides:

> When they [the diplomats] are angry, the princes tremble for fear. When they retire into private life, the world is at peace.

Fourth, as is true with so many other periods of physical conflict in world history, this was an age of feverish intellectual activity in which many schools of thought developed in a fantastic heterodoxy that soon threatened to undermine orthodox Confucianism. This aspect of the age is most significant for our discussion since it provided the stimulus for Mencius' brilliant lifelong defense of Confucianism. This is well illustrated in his reply to a disciple who asked him why he was so fond of dispute:

> Indeed, why should I be fond of disputing? But, how can I help it? . . . In ancient times, the great Yü regulated the inundating waters, and the world was returned to order. The Duke of

Chou absorbed the Yi and Ti [barbarian tribes] and drove away all ferocious animals and the people enjoyed repose. Confucius completed the *Spring and Autumn*, and rebellious ministers were struck with terror. . . . I will follow these three Sages in rectifying men's hearts, wiping out heterodox ideas, restricting their improper actions and suppressing their dissolute words. Do I do so because I love disputing? I cannot help it.

In particular, Mencius attacked Yang Chu (Chapter 5) and Mo Ti (Chapter 6) in no uncertain terms:

The words of Yang Chu and Mo Ti fill the whole world. If the people do not adopt the views of the former, they adopt those of the latter. But Yang's principle of "each one for himself" excludes the claims of the sovereign. Mo's principle of "all-embracing love" leaves out the claims of the parent. Abolition of fatherhood and princehood is the reduction of mankind to the level of wild beasts. If the doctrines of Yang and Mo are not checked, and the doctrine of Confucius is not promoted, perverse teachings will delude the people and block the way of human-heartedness and righteousness. If these are blocked, beasts will be led to devour men, and men will devour one another.

Moreover, Mencius did not take kindly to the

southern philosophers, who professed allegiance to the teachings of Shên Nung, the Divine Farmer. These people believed in the simple life even to the extent of having a sovereign labor in the field for his own food. Mencius was quick to ridicule this, pointing out that the business of government and the labor of farming could not be concurrent:

> The reason is that some kinds of business are proper to the great and others to the small. Moreover, everyone has to be supplied with the products of other men's industry. Everyone in the world would be thrown into confusion if a sovereign had to make the articles for his own use. Hence, there is the saying: "Some toil with their minds; others toil with their bodies. Those who toil with their minds govern others, while those who toil with their bodies are governed by others. Those who are governed produce food; those who govern are fed." This is a principle universally recognized.

With this chaotic world picture in mind, it is easy to understand Mencius' compulsive search for an enlightened sovereign who could provide the order and stability that the Age of Warring States longed for. But Mencius finally had to conclude:

> As a rule, in the course of five hundred years, there should arise a good sovereign. . . . According to the number of years, the time is already overdue. According to the situation of the

time, we might expect the rise of such individuals. But Heaven does not wish that there should be peace and good government in the world. If Heaven wished this, who is there besides me to bring it about?

[3]

THE DOCTRINE OF HUMAN NATURE

As an apostle of the Confucian school, Mencius naturally made *jen* the focal point of his thought. However, he introduced a modification by his claim that, for the cultivation of virtues, *jen* should be coupled with *yi* or righteousness:

What one upholds in his heart is human-heartedness; what one upholds in his conduct is righteousness.

In his effort to develop these ethical ideas, Mencius made his chief contribution to Chinese thought, his belief in the innate goodness of human nature.

Much controversy had arisen among the followers of Confucius as to the moral quality of human nature, and Mencius was the first to enunciate distinctly the doctrine that the nature of man inclines him to goodness and kindness. There were in Mencius' time three different theories on this subject. One, advanced by Kao Tzŭ, with whom Mencius had many arguments, held that human nature was neither good nor bad. Another maintained that human nature could be either good or bad, depending upon circumstances. The third stated that the nature of some men was good while that of others was bad.

There is one passage from the *Mêng Tzŭ* that serves as a general statement of the doctrine that man's nature is good:

> It is because of man's innate feelings that human nature may be considered good. If man does what is not good, his instincts are not to blame.
>
> The feeling of compassion is common to all men; so is that of shame and dislike, of modesty and yielding and of right and wrong. The feeling of compassion means human-heartedness; that of shame and dislike, righteousness; that of modesty and yielding, propriety; that of right and wrong, wisdom.
>
> Thus, human-heartedness, righteousness, propriety and wisdom are not infused into us from without, but are inherent in our nature. Sometimes we forget them because of want of reflection. As the saying goes, "Seek and you shall find; neglect and you shall lose." . . . It is said in the Poetry:
>
> Heaven creates this multitude of people;
> All things are governed by proper laws;
> Abide by the nature of man,
> And all will love the virtue of goodness.

In summary, this passage reveals three points: first,

man is good by nature and will naturally do what is good; second, man possesses four virtues: human-heartedness, righteousness, propriety and wisdom; third, Heaven creates men and their innate feelings. Each of these three points will be examined further.

One particular debate between Mencius and Kao Tzŭ illustrates the views outlined above:

> "Human nature is like the willow and righteousness like a wooden bowl," said Kao Tzŭ. "Developing human-heartedness and righteousness is like making a bowl out of the willow."
>
> To this Mencius replied: "Can you, following the nature of the willow, make out of it a bowl? And if you must deprive the willow of its nature in the process of making a bowl, then in like manner you would deprive man of his nature in the process of developing human-heartedness and righteousness. Such being the case, your words would lead all men to regard human-heartedness and righteousness as evils."

In short, Kao Tzŭ's comparison is unjust since the natural growth of the willow must be stopped in order to make a bowl out of it, while human-heartedness and righteousness are a product of man's natural development.

Again, Kao Tzŭ said:

> "Human nature is whirling water. Open an outlet to the east, and it flows to the east; open an outlet to the west, and it flows to the west.

For human nature is indifferent to good or bad, just as water is indifferent to the east or to the west."

Mencius rejoined: "Water will indeed flow indifferently to the east or west, but will it flow indifferently up or down? Human nature is disposed to goodness just as water tends to flow downward. There is no water but that it flows downward, and no man but he who shows tendency to be good. Now, by splashing water you may cause it to fly over your head; and by damming it, you may make it go uphill. But is that the nature of water? It is an external force that causes it to do so only. Likewise, when man is made to do what is not good, his nature is being forced away from its true urgings."

Moreover, Mencius saw human nature as confounded by the externals of life. The following allegory of Bull Mountain offers a good illustration of how the world spoils man's innate nature:

> The trees on the Bull Mountain were once beautiful. But being too near the capital of a great state, they were hewn down. . . . Even so, nourished by the rain and dew and with the force of growth operating day and night, the stumps sent forth fresh sprouts. But soon cattle and sheep came to browse on them, and in the end the mountain became bare again. Seeing it thus, people now imagine that it was never wooded. But is this the nature of the mountain?
> So it is with human nature. How can it be

said that man is devoid of human-heartedness and righteousness? He has only lost his good feelings in the same way that the trees have been felled. Assailed day after day, can the heart retain its goodness? Even so, nourished by the calm air of dawn and with the force of life operating day and night, man develops in his heart desires and aversions that are proper to humanity. But soon these good feelings are fettered and destroyed by the inroads of the day's activity. Thus, fettered again and again, they wither until the nourishing influence of night is no longer able to keep them alive. So in the end man reverts to a state not much different from that of birds and beasts, and seeing him thus, people imagine that man never had good feelings. But is such the nature of man?

The meaning here is quite obvious—man, like the mountain, is originally beautiful. However, under the influence of external forces, whether they be axes, animals or our daily life, man, like the mountain, finally lies deprived of his original beauty. This, of course, does not allow us to say that human nature is not good and beautiful. Mencius extended this idea to maintain that men by nature are the same, their differences being due to environment. He compared men to crops of barley that are alike but only so long as they are grown under identical circumstances.

The only exception Mencius allowed to the goodness of human nature was an indefinable area within man, which he saw as being destitute of any moral tendency and wholly passive to the shaping of environment. It is this exception that enabled Mencius to explain why men, though all essentially good, are not equal in moral achievement. For when a man's external environment is particularly harmful it develops this plastic neutral area in such ways that man's fulfillment of his goodness is interfered with.

As we have already seen in Mencius' broad statement of man's good nature, he regarded man as having certain instinctive feelings that implied the virtues that make man good. We remember that he summarized these feelings as those of compassion, shame and dislike, modesty and yielding and right and wrong. He gave the following example:

> If men suddenly see a child about to fall into a well, they will without exception experience a feeling of alarm and distress. They will feel so, not because they hope to win the gratitude of the child's parents, nor because they want to seek the praise of their neighbors, nor because they are distressed at the child's cries. From this case we may perceive that one who lacks the feeling of compassion or shame and dislike or modesty and yielding or right and wrong is not a man. The feeling of compassion is the beginning of humanheartedness; shame and dislike, the beginning of righteousness; modesty and yielding, the beginning of propriety; right and wrong, the begin-

ning of wisdom. Man has these four beginnings just as he has four limbs.

Mencius went on to conclude from this:

> Since all men have these four beginnings in themselves, let them know how to give them full development and completion. The result will be like fire that has begun to burn or a spring that has begun to find vent.

Mencius saw it as man's duty to cultivate these basic qualities, in particular, so as to achieve human-heartedness and righteousness.

> Human-heartedness is man's heart, and righteousness is man's path. Alas, for those who abandon the path and pursue it not. Alas, for those who lose the heart and seek it not! When men lose their fowl and dogs, they know to seek them. But they lose the heart and do not know to seek for it. The end of learning is nothing but the search for the lost heart.

To seek for the lost heart meant to try to recover our natural goodness. This, Mencius felt, was man's supreme duty.

Finally, going even a step beyond this duty of man to himself, Mencius was characteristically Confucian in his concern for the interplay among human beings. Thus, it would not be enough to recover our own natural goodness; we have a responsibility to develop and extend it so that it will be a blessing for all.

> Treat the aged in your family as they should be treated, and extend this treatment to the aged of other people's families. Treat the young in your family as they should be treated, and extend this treatment to the young of other people's families.

Mencius called this "extending one's good heart to include others," and he viewed it as the ultimate development of *jen*.

[4]

POLITICS, PRINCIPLES AND POLICIES

Like Confucius, Mencius was much concerned with achieving good government—what he called "humane" government. True to the traditions of the Confucian school, he maintained that good government depends not upon brute force but on the example set by the ruler. Two types of government are possible according to Mencius:

> That which depends on force and discredits human-heartedness is the "tyrant's rule" [*pa*] . . . that which abides by virtue and practices human-heartedness is the "kingly way" [*wang*]. . . . But when one subdues men by force, they do not sub-

mit to him in their hearts—they submit because they cannot resist. When one subdues men by virtue, they are pleased in their hearts and submit of their own accord.

Mencius' conclusions here were to be expected, not just because he was Confucius' heir, but also because of the chaotic world he knew. Reacting to his environment, he deduced his theory of government from his general doctrine that human nature is good:

All men have a heart which cannot bear to see the sufferings of others. The ancient kings had this compassionate heart, and they therefore had likewise a compassionate government. Then, the rule of the world was as easy as turning things around in the palm of one's hand.

Growing out of this concept of "humane" government was Mencius' recognition of the importance of the role of the people in government.

The people rank highest in a state; the spirits of the grain come next; and the sovereign is of least account.

Good government should work upward from the people instead of downward from the ruling class. The people are not only the root but also the final judge of government. Mencius granted the "Mandate of Heaven" doctrine found in the *Book of History,* which pictures the emperor as the son of Heaven and the first servant of the state. However, he quoted further from the *History* in recalling that Heaven "has no fixed will but sees with the people's eyes and hears with the people's ears." Thus, the opinion of the people is of supreme significance, and the people have the right to depose a wicked king. It is worth remarking that this antedates John Locke's theories about the consent of the governed and the right of revolution by about 2000 years.

As far as the ruler's responsibilities are concerned, Mencius outlined them generally in speaking to King Hui of Liang:

> If Your Majesty practices "humane" government, thus abating severe penalty, diminishing taxes and levies, causing farms to be attended with care and industry, enabling the strong-bodied during leisure days to cultivate filial piety, fraternal love, loyalty and honesty . . . your people will be capable of being employed with wooden staffs to oppose the strong nail and sharp weapons of [enemy] troops.

More specifically, the ruler's main functions could be broken down as: first, that of enriching the people generally, of improving their over-all welfare; second, that of educating the people—in ceremonial rites, in social order and in national loyalty. These functions or ideal policies are discussed in the following paragraphs.

Mencius required that a ruler should above all seek

to enrich the people, because virtue and peace would not come so long as hunger and cold were the order of the day:

> The people cannot live without water and fire. Yet, if you knock at a man's door in the evening and ask for water and fire, no man will refuse to give them. Such is the abundance of these things. . . . When food supplies are as abundant as water and fire, how shall the people be other than virtuous?

The measures that Mencius envisioned for achieving this ideal were not so unrealistic as we might at first suspect:

> If the seasons for farming are not interfered with, there will be more grain than can be consumed. If close-meshed nets are not allowed in the pools and lakes, there will be more fish and turtles than can be consumed. If the axes and hatchets are brought to the forest only at the proper time, there will be more timber than can be used. When they have more grain and fish than they can eat and more timber than they can use, the people will be able to feed the living and bury the dead without undue worry and vexation. To ensure this for the people is the first duty of the good government.

In agriculture, Mencius wanted to restore the *ching-t'ien* or "well-field" system, in which arable land was divided into squares of nine hundred *mu* (the size of the ancient *mu* is not known; the modern one is about one-third of an acre), each square being assigned to eight families after having been plotted in a form resembling the Chinese character for "well" or *ching*. The eight outer plots were cultivated by the individual families; the central one mutually, but its produce was reserved for the state in lieu of taxes. This system had broken down with the end of the Chou period and had been replaced by personal land ownership, which as a matter of fact was to last over the centuries until the accession of the Communists.

With his goal of individual prosperity in mind, Mencius also opposed the oppressive taxation of the time—especially burdensome, as we have seen, because of the need for financing the ceaseless wars. He recognized the necessity for taxation but criticized the degree and forms it had assumed. He cited three methods that had been or were then practiced: the tax under the ancient Hsia dynasty, really a tribute; the Yin dynasty's contribution, made in the form of mutual aid; and the Chou assessment for the government. Of the three, Mencius seemed to favor that of Yin at the expense of the Chou:

> ... there is no better system than that of mutual aid and no worse than that of taxing. By the latter, the regular amount is fixed by taking an average of several years. As a result, in the good years, when the grain lies about in abundance, much may be taken without being oppressive, and the actual amount is small. But in bad years, when

the produce is not enough even to pay for the manuring, this system still requires the taking of the full amount. Thus, the ruler causes his people to toil throughout the year without even the reward of adequate nourishment.

Still further, Mencius named hempen cloth and silk, grain and personal service as the proper things for taxation. But he stressed that the prince "should raise one of these per year, deferring the other two."

As far as education was concerned, Mencius merely pointed out that proper instruction and good government go hand in hand.

> Kindly words do not touch men so profoundly as kindly deeds. Likewise, good government does not hold people so firmly as good education. For good government produces only awe in the people's minds, while good education inspires love. Good government gains the people's wealth, while good education gains their hearts.

Mencius saw education as the end of good government just as wealth is the origin of government. With wisdom that we can well profit from, he recognized solid economic well-being as not enough of itself—the people must be taught other things:

> Men possess a moral nature. If they are well fed, warmly clad and comfortably lodged, without being properly educated, they become like beasts.

[5]

AN ESTIMATE

Much of what was said in summarizing Confucius can be applied here—with several striking exceptions. First, while both were interested primarily in good government, Mencius insisted that such government should function for, and with the consent of, the people: thus, "The people rank highest in a state . . . the sovereign is of last account." Confucius had made the sovereign an all-powerful overlord, and he had granted only that the people's confidence in their ruler was important. In the end, Mencius took an entirely opposite position:

> There is only one way to hold imperial rule: hold the people. There is only one way to hold their hearts: provide them with what they like and do not impose on them what they loathe.

Second, and as the next logical step, Mencius assigned the people, and the ministers as well, the right to depose a wicked king. Confucius had defined only a static, unchanging relationship:

> Let the ruler be ruler; the minister, minister; the father, father; and the son, son.[2]

For championing this revolutionary concept, Mencius

---
[2] *Analects,* XII, 11.

can almost be regarded as a democrat in the modern sense.

Third, although both accepted the view that good government was dependent on material and spiritual well-being, Mencius was, as we have seen, far more specific than his master. Thus, for him, it was not enough to say that people should be made prosperous and then educated. Rather, he expounded his beliefs in the specific areas mentioned above, such as the "well-field" system of farming, the control of taxes, conservation, etc.

Finally, Mencius made the doctrine of the goodness of human nature the focal point of his system where, to Confucius, human-heartedness had been of prime importance. It is in this doctrine, with its stress on the goodness of man, that Mencius stands out as a figure of gigantic importance—a worthy successor to the immortal Sage.

Lao Tzŭ

"When the Sage acts, he rests in the quietism of *wu wei*. When he teaches, he practices the precept of silence."
Tao Tê Ching, II, 7.

3. Lao Tzŭ

Lao Tzŭ (Old Master) was the earliest prominent Taoist philosopher—really the founder of Taoism, also known as Laoism. He lived in the sixth century B.C. and was contemporary with, but older than, Confucius. In ancient times, his fame was as great as that of Confucius, and his teachings were no less influential. However, the two differed as widely as Plato from Aristotle. Lao Tzŭ's vast impact is attested to by the fact that in time he came to be regarded as the supreme god of Taoism—an interesting contradiction in terms since Lao Tzŭ himself was an atheist who would have regarded the formation of a religion and the naming of gods as contrary to his teachings.

[1]

LIFE AND WRITINGS

Some still regard Lao Tzŭ, also known as Lao Tan, as merely a mythological figure with a curious assortment of apocryphal stories and fantastic legends surrounding his name. However, on the basis of the short biography in the *Shih Chi* or *Historical Records* of Ssŭ-ma Ch'ien, the Herodotus of China who lived in the second century B.C., most now do accept his historical authenticity, granting the unfortunate lack of facts about him.

Lao Tzŭ means "old master" and is therefore a title rather than a name. The old master's real name was Lai Tan, but he was respectfully addressed as Lai Tzŭ. And in later years the word *lao* or "old" was added, thus, Lao Lai Tzŭ. This was abbreviated to Lao Tzŭ or Lao Tan.

Lao Tzŭ is said to have been keeper of the imperial archives in the royal capital at Lo, and, as we saw in Chapter 1, he is supposed to have met Confucius when the latter visited the Chou capital. If, in fact, the two ever did meet it is probable that they found themselves at odds since their views differed so strongly. Where Confucius was humanistic and concerned with social relations, Lao Tzŭ taught a philosophy that is essentially naturalistic and antisocial. Where the Sage's goal lay in influencing some enlightened sovereign, Lao Tzŭ's was simply that of withdrawing from all thought of sovereigns and rule.

Some of the differences between the two great philosophers can be explained on the basis of their geographical origins. We have already observed the strong influence of the ritualistic Chou culture that naturally fell upon Confucius as a resident of Lu. Lao Tzŭ, however, was born in the state of Chan (modern Honan), which was later absorbed by the big Yangtzu state of Ch'u, whence came most of the Taoist teachers. The Chans were the people of Yin (Shang), a dynasty that preceded the Chou and which had a culture of naturalistic simplicity. Thus, in a sense, the opposition between Confucianism and Taoism is an extension of the early differences between the Chou and Shang cultures.

Unlike Confucius, who traveled from state to state campaigning for political reform, Lao Tzŭ preferred to do his work in anonymity, practicing the *Tao* of the universe. Apparently he remained in his position at Lo for a considerable period until the time when he recognized the signs of decay in the Chou house. At first, he merely resigned, but dismayed at the increasing disintegration and chaos, he shortly went into exile. Traditionally, it is held that he was stopped at the frontier and requested to commit to writing the philosophy he had worked out. He is supposed to have remained there long enough to do this, setting his teachings down in two parts, *Tao* and *Tê*, that extend for five thousand words. After that he disappeared, and nothing further is known of him although he is supposed to have lived in seclusion to a great age.

As indicated, this is the traditional view, with Lao Tzŭ honored as the author of the first philosophical work in Chinese history. Another view, one which lays stress on some anachronisms and repeated passages, holds the entire work to be a forgery of the Han dynasty. Finally, those modern scholars particularly trained in textual criticism maintain that, even if a historical figure named Lao Tzŭ did live in the age of the *Spring and Autumn Annals* (722–481 B.C.), he did not write the *Tao Tê Ching*, since internal evidence of content and style suggests a much later composition—specifically, in the Age of Warring States (480–222 B.C.).

Not one of these theories has been conclusively established, and this is not the place to undertake an extended analysis of the controversy. However, it is worthwhile to mention in passing a common-sense explanation of the difficulty: namely, that the *Tao Tê Ching* was compiled during the Age of Warring States by Lao Tzŭ's disciples, who made free use of the written memorials about their master and of actual statements they had heard him make. That this solution to the controversy is most reasonable becomes especially apparent if we recall that the Confucian *Analects* and a number of other ancient classics were compiled in just this fashion. This theory also explains why in these ancient works there is no connection between one paragraph and the next, each statement apparently intended as complete in itself. This would indeed be the case if a number of persons had composed a work.

Probably the most pertinent thing that can be said in this connection is that, apart from considerations of exact authorship, it is generally conceded that most of the book correctly represents the philosophy of the original Lao Tzŭ. Certainly, the book is in line with what we would expect Taoist thought to be just before the time of Confucius. The earliest philosophers in China, as elsewhere, had been naturalists ever looking outward upon the external world instead of inward upon themselves. It was not until approximately the sixth century B.C. that philosophy began to deal with the inward problems of man, life, human destiny and ethics. The emergence and crystallization of this point of view, i.e., the transition from naturalism to humanism, can be pinpointed in the figure of Confucius. The *Tao Tê Ching* stands at the threshold of this emergence. Thus, probably the most accurate thing to say of the book is that it is the product of not one but many hands, but that it correctly represents the philosophy of Lao Tzŭ, who lived in the period immediately prior to Confucius.

The book consisted of two parts, *Tao* and *Tê*, until the time of Emperor Ching (156–141 B.C.) of the Han dynasty when it was combined into one volume under the title we now know, *Tao Tê Ching*. However, Emperor Hsüan Chung (713–755 A.D.) of the T'ang dynasty again divided the book into two volumes—the *Tao Ching* and the *Tê Ching*. Although the original had no internal subdivisions, the work was later divided into chapters. Their number varies from fifty-five to eighty-one.

[2]

THE CONCEPTION OF TAO

Man conforms to Earth;
Earth conforms to Heaven;
Heaven conforms to Tao;
And Tao *conforms to the way of Nature.**

This is the general outline of Lao Tzŭ's system. By Nature is meant all that happens in the universe; that

---

*All extracts in this chapter are from the *Tao Tê Ching*, unless otherwise noted.

is, the totality of the spontaneity of things—the absolute freedom from artificiality. Thus, when things are allowed to take their natural course, they move with perfection and harmony because they then do not hinder *Tao* in its natural and spontaneous operation as the first principle of the universe. This is known as the way of *wu wei* (doing nothing) or, a step further, the way of *wei wu wei* (doing everything by doing nothing).

> *Tao* invariably does nothing, and yet there is nothing that is not done.

This doctrine of *wu wei* is the central thesis of Lao Tzŭ's system.

Two points follow from this conception. First, in the *History* and the *Poetry*, Heaven is personified as *Shang Ti* or the "Supreme Being," providing for the wants of men and rewarding them according to their deeds. Lao Tzŭ, however, denied the existence of *Shang Ti* and held that Heaven, instead of being divine, merely conforms to *Tao*. Here Lao Tzŭ was an atheist.

The second point is that his philosophy is an idealization of nature and a depreciation of art. According to Lao Tzŭ, man is originally happy but suffers as a result of changes brought on by society. The best way to be happy is to undo the present artificial civilization and to live in tranquil communion with nature among forests and streams and hills. In terms that draw an interesting distinction between knowledge and *Tao*, the return to nature is accomplished as follows:

By the pursuit of knowledge, one gains day by
  day;
By the pursuit of *Tao*, one loses day by day.
One will lose and keep losing until one attains the
  quietism of *wu wei*.
Do nothing, and there is nothing that is not done.
By doing nothing, one wins the world.
But when one grasps, the world is beyond his win-
  ning.

Obviously, the term *Tao* is of critical importance. The opening sentence of the *Tao Tê Ching* reads:

The *Tao* that can be expressed in words is not
  the eternal *Tao*.
The name that can be named is not the abiding
  name.

According to Lao Tzŭ, there was something that preceded the birth of the universe. This something is designated as *Tao*, which, in reality, is not a name. The *Tao*, therefore, cannot be designated in words, nor can it be perceived by physical senses.

Because the eye gazes but never sees it, it is called
  yi.
Because the ear listens but never hears it, it is
  called *hsi*.
Because the hand reaches but never grasps it, it is
  called *wei*.
These three cannot be further scrutinized, for
  they blend into the One.

Thus, the *Tao* is invisible, inaudible and impalpable; but it remains eternal, ineffable and culminates in the state of nonbeing. The *Tao* is an invariable law underlying the changing phenomena of the universe. It is eternal, all-pervasive, inexhaustible in its use and fathomless like the fountainhead of all things. That is why the *Tao*, which follows the way of Nature, is itself followed by Heaven, Earth and Man.

Tao is better understood in the light of *Tê*. The word *Tê* as used in the *Tao Tê Ching* is a much more comprehensive concept than mere virtue as known to the Confucian school. The *Tao* is that by which all things come to be. But in this process of coming to be, each individual thing obtains something from the universal *Tao*, and this something is called *Tê*. Hence, the *Tê* is a concept connoting the natural state of things. Therefore, the *Tê* of a thing is what the thing naturally *is*.

The *Tao* is the ultimate element of life, and man should aspire to live in conformity with it. The *Tê* is the operating force of life, and life can be nourished and enriched by it. Both *Tao* and *Tê* are of Nature, in the sense of spontaneity. Just as the totality of the spontaneity of all things in the universe is called *Tao*, so the totality of spontaneity of each individual thing is called *Tê*. It is the *Tao* by which all things come to be, and it is the *Tê* by which they are what they are. That is why "all things esteem the *Tao* and honor the *Tê*."

From the conception of *Tao* just presented, we note that when Lao Tzŭ said that the *Tao* produces all things, he meant nothing more than the fact that it allows them to produce themselves, naturally and spontaneously. Thus, the *Tao* does nothing. But the *Tao* "gives life to things . . . accomplishes all . . . nourishes all." The *Tao* does everything. Once again:

> The *Tao* invariably does nothing and yet there is nothing that is not done.

That is the way of *wei wu wei*.

[3]

THE EVOLUTION OF THE UNIVERSE

There are three points to be remembered in connection with the idea of *Tao* as applied to the evolution of the universe.

The first is stated as follows:

> All things in the world come into being from *yu* [being].
> *Yu* comes into being from *wu* [nonbeing].

In other words, *wu* denotes the state that existed before the birth of Heaven and Earth; *yu* that state when things began to have separate existence. The transition from *wu* to *yu* was brought about by the cosmic force, which, as we expect, is *Tao*. *Tao* is wrapped in cosmic mystery, but is the sole source of life, form, substance and essence.

> The all-embracing *Tê* echoes the *Tao*.
> The *Tao* itself is vague and impalpable.

> Though vague and impalpable, within is Form.
> Though impalpable and vague, within is Substance.
> Though profound and obscure, within is Essence.
> Its essence is real and embedded in truth.

Lao Tzŭ also explained the evolutionary process by stating that the *Tao* generates "One" or the Great Ultimate. "One," in turn, produces "Two," or *yin* and *yang,* the prime forces in the universe constituting a kind of dualism. *Yin* is the negative or passive force; *yang,* the positive or active. The interaction of these two leads to life, as designated by "Three," out of which arise all things.

The second point is that in the process of evolution, every phenomenon involves its opposite or contradictory or negative side. So life is followed by death, light by darkness and good by evil.

> Where the world perceives beauty, ugliness also exists;
> Where the world perceives good, evil also exists:
> Therefore, being and nonbeing involve each other; difficulty and ease involve each other.
> The long and the short are related; the high and the low are related, too.

Thus, the universe is composed of pairs or opposites whose fundamental character is that they are made up of being and nonbeing. The evolution of the universe, all changes, all motions, are thus the passage of nonbeing into being, of nothing into something. But though things are ever changeable and changing, the laws that govern change are themselves constant.

Among these laws, the most fundamental is that "Reversion is the motion of the *Tao*," that is, if any movement goes to its extreme of development, it necessarily executes a reversion. For instance:

> Calamity will promote blessing; blessing, too, underlies calamity ....
> The right may turn out to be wrong ....
> The good may turn out to be evil.

This is not only true of human affairs, but is the essential evolutionary process of the universe as a whole.

> The way of Heaven is like a stretching bow:
> When the upper part is leveled, the lower part is raised up.
> When the excess is diminished, the deficiency is replenished.

Lao Tzǔ termed this invariable law of nature *ch'ang* or "Normality." Were the universe not to conform to the normality of nature, it would cease to function. For the sun to rise from the west and set in the east would indeed be abnormal. But nature never tries such a thing because it is contrary to the *Tao*. So Lao Tzǔ said:

> Knowing Normality, a man is all-embracing.
> Being all-embracing, he is selfless.
> Being selfless, he is supreme.

Being supreme, he is divine.
Being divine, he is with *Tao*.
With *Tao*, he is everlasting.

The third point, as a necessary corollary to the doctrine of *wu wei*, is that all things in the universe take their natural course. The sun shines, and water flows because it is in their nature to do so. Plants and trees grow and die because it is in their nature to do so. Lao Tzŭ denied the existence of a Supreme Being who controls the motion of the universe. He held that Heaven and Earth, signifying the Supreme Being, have nothing to do with the growth and development of things, for all things come into being through a natural course. Consequently Lao Tzŭ said:

The universe is amoral.

The innate quality of all that happens is an invariable natural spontaneity, such as the brilliance of the sun and the moon, the fluidity of water and the growth of plants. The universe as a whole is spontaneity itself, so it has no desire or wish to be moral. It simply leaves all things to take their natural course.

However, as already indicated, Lao Tzŭ did not deny that in the universe there is a power at work whose nature is inscrutable. That power is in fact the *Tao*, which can be characterized by its quietude of power, its production without possession, action without self-assertion, development without domination. *Tao* is impersonal and never conscious of its own being. Although to its being all things owe their existence, it is itself without form and void. As a matter of fact, *Tao* did not and could not produce the universe. When we say that *Tao* produces the universe, we simply mean that the universe produces itself spontaneously and naturally. Since the universe does this, it will take its natural and spontaneous course. This is the basis of Lao Tzŭ's doctrine of *wu wei*.

Admittedly, these ideas, since they are dependent on at least some perception of the meaning of *Tao*, are difficult to understand. Lao Tzŭ recognized this:

> Men of the highest caliber, hearing of the *Tao*, earnestly practice it.
> Average men, hearing of the *Tao*, are not interested in it.
> Vulgar men, hearing of the *Tao*, laugh loudly at it.
> Indeed, if these men did not laugh, it could not be the *Tao*.

[4]

THE IDEAL OF LIFE

Lao Tzŭ's ideal of life is itself based on the doctrine of *wu wei*. He taught not only the virtue of nonaction but also that of nonbeing. Taking as illustrations the holes of a wheel, the hollowness of a clay vessel and the interior of a house, in all of which value comes from emptiness, he stated his thesis:

By the existence of things we profit;
By the nonexistence of things we are served.

Lao Tzŭ exalted the "Spirit of Valley," its hollowness being symbolic of the Taoist void; and he called it "the Mystic Female," that is, the foremost principle of life, because the female conquers the world by being soft and weak, humble and low. Hence Lao Tzŭ said:

A man, when alive, is supple and pliant; but in death he is stiff and cold;
Similarly, all things—grass and trees, for example—when alive, are flexible and soft; whereas dead, they are dry and brittle.
Therefore, to be stiff and cold is the way of death; to be supple and soft is the way of life.
The stiff weapon may break, just as a rigid tree may crack.
The strong and mighty topple from their places; the soft and supple rise above them.

Lao Tzŭ saw in the behavior of water a pattern for his natural way of life:

Nothing in the world is more supple and soft than water,
But even the most hard and stiff cannot overcome it.

It seemed to him that on the surface, water, being soft, yielding and fluid, is female in quality; but that when it flows down from the mountains, forming great rivers and cutting through rocks and barriers effortlessly and naturally, it is male. Hence, water, though possessed of male strength, abides by its "meekness of the female," to accomplish what it seeks. Lao Tzŭ concluded:

Meekness is the way of the Tao.

Unfortunately, however, man goes contrary to the way of *Tao* by doing what nature avoids. Himself a part of nature's vast pattern of things, man persists in getting away from nature's invariable law. That is why the universe functions smoothly and harmoniously in the endless span of time and space, whereas man encounters all the ills and pains of life. According to Lao Tzŭ, man is originally happy, but he suffers through his own effort to control his destiny, thereby impeding the natural flow of spontaneity. The best way to be happy is to live true to nature and revert to the state of pristine simplicity. Lao Tzŭ expressed his ideal when he spoke of the ancients who

... attuning themselves with the *Tao*, possessed a subtle and penetrating wisdom ... but they were submissive and humble like melting ice. Their manner was simple and pure as the unhewn block [*p'u*]. Their minds were broad and deep like open valleys. Their views were impartial and tolerant like troubled waters.

With such ideas of naturalism and revolt against all human conventions and institutions, it was inevitable that Lao Tzŭ despised the Confucian virtues of human-heartedness and righteousness. In fact, he attributed man's degeneration from *Tao* and *Tê* to these virtues:

> Therefore, when *Tao* is lost, there is *Tê*.
> When the *Tê* is lost, there is humanity.
> When humanity is lost, there is righteousness.
> When righteousness is lost, there is propriety.
> The rules of propriety are brought about by the lack of loyalty and good faith and by the prevalence of confusion.

Likewise, Lao Tzŭ held knowledge to be useless; action, superfluous; desire, harmful; and glory and wealth, worthless. All these things are matters of human choice, not natural growth; they are the artificial result, not the natural course. A man may live true to nature, and nature may point him to happiness; but his artificial knowledge and desire may get the upper hand and lead him astray.

> The five colors blind the eye.
> The five sounds deafen the ear.
> The five flavors impair the taste.
> The pursuit of pleasures deranges the mind.
> The love of treasures perverts conduct.

Therefore, the wise man, in order to avoid the faults of the people, is free from desire, does not covet rarities and does not acquire learning. He leaves all things to their natural course.

It was the passivity of the process of nature that most impressed Lao Tzŭ. As a part of the universe, man shares with other things, living and lifeless, the same quality of naturalness. Just as Heaven and Earth attain complete harmony and order only by attuning themselves to *Tao*, so can man attain the highest well-being only by arriving at thorough conformity with *Tao*. But man has used whatever power he possesses to choose his own way and build his social habits in accordance with his insignificant mortal faculties rather than the eternal principles of the great *Tao*. Hence have sprung all the ills and pains of man, in the midst of the artificial civilization he has formed. Therefore, Lao Tzŭ, yielding himself to *Tao*, did not struggle to assert himself—nor did he strive for superiority in any way. Indeed, he viewed the mental state of infancy as a standard for the natural way of life. He felt that infants, having limited knowledge and few desires, and being untarnished by worldly contact, are closer to *Tao* than grownups.

[5]

THE THEORY OF GOVERNMENT

The doctrine of *wu wei* was to govern the conduct of government as well as the personal life. Lao Tzŭ was born into the age of social and political upset we have discussed. He attributed these ills to two things: first, the complexity of social and political institutions; second, the activities of the ruling classes. He went to the extreme of proclaiming laws, regulations, ceremonies and even ethical codes as anathema since he felt they served only to encourage the people to violate them.

> The more restrictions and prohibitions there are in the world, the poorer the people will become.
> The more sharp weapons the people possess, the more troubled the state will be.
> The more craft and cunning the people have, the more pernicious connivings will they invent.
> The more laws and edicts that are imposed, the more thieves and bandits there will be.

The first act of the ruler, then, should be to remove all such causes of social disorder and political confusion.

> Banish wisdom, discard knowledge, and the people will be benefited a hundredfold.
> Banish human-heartedness, discard righteousness, and the people will again become filial and affectionate.
> Banish skill, discard profit, and thieves and robbers will no longer exist.

Likewise, the best way to govern is

> . . . to empty the people's hearts, but fill their stomachs; to weaken their wills, but to strengthen

their bones ... to make the people without knowledge and desire, and the sly without craft.

As to the reasons for this political theory, Lao Tzŭ said:

> The people suffer hunger because the rulers levy too many taxes.
> The people are hard to govern because the rulers meddle with them.
> The people risk death because they worry too much about life.

Accordingly, the rulers, if versed in *Tao*, would not enlighten the people by their rule but have them held in "ignorance." (Here, the word "ignorance" is a translation of the Chinese *yu*, which means ignorance in the sense of simplicity and innocence.) Simplicity and innocence are the characteristics that every man should retain. Therefore, *yu*, as conceived in the teachings of Lao Tzŭ, is not a vice but a great virtue.

It is obvious that the only principle of government consistent with the teachings of Lao Tzŭ is that of laissez faire, the minimum of organization and of regulations. Lao Tzŭ said:

> Govern a large country as you would cook a small fish.

To cook a small fish, as we know, needs little time and skill. Similarly, to govern a large country would be just as easy and simple if the ruler would only let his people alone.

So the wise man says: "So long as I do nothing,
the people are reformed of themselves.

So long as I love quietude, the people are righteous of themselves.

So long as I make no effort, the people grow rich by themselves.

So long as I am free from desire, the people are simple and honest in themselves."

Were this laissez-faire policy allowed to prevail in politics, an ideal community would eventually come into being. The following passage offers a good picture of the ideal community:

The ideal state is small; its people, few.

They do not use tools and implements even though available.

They avoid risks of death and do not emigrate to distant countries.

Thus, although there are carriages and boats, no one rides in them.

Though there are weapons of war, no one displays them. . . .

The people are content with their food, satisfied with their clothing, peaceful in their dwellings and happy with their common lot.

Neighbor lands are juxtaposed so that each may hear the other's barking dogs and crowing cocks.

To the end of their days, the people never care to come or go.

This was Lao Tzŭ's utopia.

[6]

AN ESTIMATE

Probably the best way to form a just estimate of Lao Tzŭ is by distinguishing between Taoism and Confucianism. These two systems represent opposite views in regard to the function of *Tao*. According to Lao Tzŭ, *Tao* is "doing by doing nothing." In order to be "doing by doing nothing," he denied all that is done by doing. Hence, he denounced civilization and knowledge and exalted the primitive and instinctual. According to Confucius, however, *Tao* is "doing for nothing." In doing, we must consciously do something for nothing since we must enjoy the doing itself. Thus, whereas Lao Tzŭ idealized nature and attributed all evils to conventions and institutions, Confucius emphasized the value of culture while teaching the pursuance of nature. In short, in Lao Tzŭ's system, there is nothing but exaltation of *Tao* at the expense of *li* (rites), of which the Confucian school was the bulwark.

Second, these two systems have different interpretations of man's relation to things. Lao Tzŭ conceived no dividing line between things and man. His thought is monistic and attempts to explain the union of the individual with the whole. It is based on the principle that all is merged into the whole or *Tao*. Hence, there can be no distinction between man and things, for all arise from the One that is *Tao*.

Confucius not only accepted a division between

things and man but also attached the paramount importance to humanity. It was not the riddle of the universe but the riddle of human life that made him ponder. Thus, where the spirit of Lao Tzŭ is idealistic and of little practical use, that of Confucius is practical and humanistic.

Third, these two systems contrast in their conceptions of Heaven. According to Lao Tzŭ, *Tao* is prior to Heaven, for *Tao* is the all-embracing first principle for the universe. But Confucius seemed equivocal in his statement about the conception of Heaven. Although he did not conceive Heaven as the Creator, he recognized it as supreme. Among the things of which Confucius stood in constant awe, the first was Heaven's ordinance. He held that Heaven was an active force interfering in human affairs.

Lao Tzŭ and Confucius resembled each other in only one important respect. Both held the doctrine of the golden mean and employed the invariable law of nature as the principal supporting argument for this doctrine—if any movement goes to its extreme of development, it necessarily reverts to its opposite. "Never too much" was the maxim for both.

Lao Tzŭ's philosophy of *wu wei* was also derived from this invariable law. *Wu wei* is by no means entirely negative in the sense of total absence of activity. What it really means is "not overdoing." By overdoing, one risks getting the opposite of what one wants. Similarly, Lao Tzŭ's philosophy teaches that we must be meek, humble and easily content. To be content is the way to preserve our strength and be strong.

In spite of this simplicity, the application of Lao

Tzŭ's philosophy of *wu wei* is difficult. How could we bring about peace and happiness in the lives and relationships of men if we were not to work for these ends? What would happen to the world if we were to abolish all social and political institutions? We cannot undo the present civilization first and then institute a state of pristine simplicity. Moreover, it is far from right to say that the utopia of mankind is the simplicity of the past. With the belief in progress we have come to hold that the ideal community is to be created in the promising future, not in the ruins of the dead past. In spite of all this, we would agree with Lao Tzŭ that there is much worth in the thought that excessive government is dangerous, and that simplicity, even in the political sphere, is an ideal to be sought— though difficult to achieve.

Lao Tzŭ has much to offer us. He shows the folly of self-seeking and the effectiveness of *wu wei* in bringing human relations to pass, naturally and simply. And he gave us a picture of an ideal community. Whether this simple life is practical and whether the theory of *wu wei* is sound are questions still to be answered.

"Chuang Chou [i.e., Chuang Tzǔ] dreamed that he was a butterfly, fluttering about—to all intents and purposes a butterfly. It did not know that it was Chuang Chou. Suddenly, he awoke and there he was Chuang Chou again. . . ."
Chuang Tzǔ, Ch. 2.

4. Chuang Tzŭ

If Confucius is indebted for the popularization of his doctrines to Mencius, Lao Tzŭ must be regarded as even more indebted in the same way to the romantic mystic Chuang Tzŭ. One of the most brilliant and delightful characters among the philosophers of China, he would probably have won for himself a still greater reputation than that which he enjoys but for the dominance of Confucianism. While he was true to Taoist teaching in its *Tao* centrality, he extended the system and carried his own speculations into regions never dreamed of by Lao Tzŭ. His philosophy idealizes the state of nature and favors anarchistic individualism, and it revolts against conventions and institutions with, ultimately, a denial of all the benefits produced by civilization.

[1]

LIFE AND TEACHINGS

Chuang Chou, better known as Chuang Tzŭ (*c.* 369–*c.* 286 B.C.), was the most brilliant of the early Taoists. He was greatly revered for the depth of his intellect, the beauty of his literary style and the sublimity of his personality. Hence, all kinds of legends grew up concerning his life, and he was even credited with the performance of miracles. But all such fantastic legends seem to have stemmed from nothing more than some paradoxical passages in his writings.

Not much is known of his life. He was a native of the small state of Mêng on the border between the present Shantung and Honan provinces. He held a petty official's post in his native state for a short period. But being a naturalist in thought, he could not accommodate himself to political life. His disgust with the disordered life of the time grew until he retired into seclusion and cut himself off from world affairs. According to one story, Chuang Tzŭ was fishing in the P'u river when two messengers came from the Prince of Ch'u to offer him the premiership of the state. But Chuang Tzŭ declined, saying that he much preferred to be a live tortoise wagging its tail in the mud than a dead one venerated in a golden casket in the king's ancestral shrine.

Chuang Tzŭ bequeathed his teachings in a book bearing his name. This book has rarely been surpassed for beauty of style and felicity of expression. Chuang Tzŭ's text as it now stands consists of thirty-three chapters, which were most probably compiled by Kuo Hsiang, Chuang Tzŭ's great commentator of the third century A.D. Because of the frequent repetitions and many interpolations there is much dispute over what Chuang Tzŭ actually wrote, and much attributed to him is said to be spurious. However, those chapters representing the naturalistic aspects of Taoism cannot be far wrong, even though they may not all have been written by Chuang Tzŭ himself. These chapters reveal that Chuang Tzŭ's philosophy falls into three divisions: metaphysics, ethics and knowledge.

[2]

METAPHYSICS

Chuang Tzŭ conceived of *Tao* as the life force of all things:

> *Tao* has reality and evidence but no action and form. It may be transmitted, yet not possessed. It existed before Heaven and Earth and lasts forever. It caused spirits and gods to be divine and Heaven and Earth to be produced. It is above the zenith, yet not high; it is below the nadir, yet not low. It is prior to Heaven and Earth, yet has no duration.*

But how can *Tao* cause the spirits and gods to be divine, and Heaven and Earth to be produced? In fact, *Tao* did not and could not cause the spirits and gods to be divine, but they were divine of themselves. This means that *Tao* caused them to be divine by not causing them. And again, *Tao* did not produce Heaven and Earth. They produced themselves. *Tao* produced them by not producing them. This is the basis of *wei wu wei* (doing everything by doing nothing).

---
*All extracts in this chapter are from the *Chuang Tzŭ*, unless otherwise noted.

Next, *Tao* embodies all things:

> *Tao* is not too small for the greatest, nor too great for the smallest. Thus, all things are embodied therein. Wide, indeed, is its boundless capacity; unfathomable, its depth.

Still further:

> *Tao* is without beginning, without end.

This last remark was deeply characteristic. Chuang Tzŭ's concern with the transitory nature of the world resulted in an effort to find the eternal amid the shifting, the abiding and permanent among the changing. *Tao*, as the eternal constant, was Chuang Tzŭ's solution.

Moreover, *Tao* is omnipresent: "There is nowhere where it is not," Chuang Tzŭ said. And from the standpoint of *Tao*, all things are one: positive and negative, subjective and objective, good and evil, life and death—all become indistinct, as water in water. In other words, by ignoring the distinction of contraries, all things are embraced in the ubiquitous *Tao*.

And finally, *Tao* is invisible, inaudible and impalpable:

> *Tao* cannot be heard; if heard, it is not *Tao*.
> *Tao* cannot be seen; if seen, it is not *Tao*.
> *Tao* cannot be spoken; if spoken, it is not *Tao*.

The essence of following *Tao* is to see nothing, hear

nothing and do nothing. In short, nothingness or nonbeing is the essence of *Tao*. This is the basic teaching of Chuang Tzŭ and also that of Lao Tzŭ.

In the application of the conception of the eternal and omnipresent *Tao* to the process of the evolution of the universe, there are three points to be considered.

First, all that happens in the universe is transitory and illusory; there is no absolute reality. Chuang Tzŭ said:

> If a canoe is placed in the crevice of a mountain that is surrounded by a lake, this is supposed to be safe enough. But at midnight a strong man may come and carry away the canoe on his back. Man is blind to see that no matter how things are concealed, there will always be a chance of losing them.

Thus, what is thought to be safe is not always so; there is no absolute safety. And this is the same as saying that what appears to our senses is merely illusory, that there is no absolute reality.

Secondly, the universe is composed of pairs of opposites such as positive and negative, subjective and objective, being and nonbeing, life and death, etc. But from the standpoint of *Tao,* all these opposites involve each other in a never-ceasing process. Thus, in the process of evolution, every phenomenon cannot exclude its negation.

When there is life, there is death; and when there

is death, there is life. When there is possibility, there is impossibility; and when there is impossibility, there is possibility. Because there is right, there is wrong. Because there is wrong, there is right.

According to Chuang Tzŭ, things originate in the cycle of change out of preceding states of existence just as the seasons mutually produce and destroy each other without end.

And thirdly, as already suggested, all things in the universe are embraced in the Infinite. The Infinite is a state in the circle of existence, the process of reverse evolution in which "all things arise out of the Infinite and return to the Infinite." The succession of growth and decay, of increase and decrease, goes in a cycle, each end becoming a new beginning.

[3]

ETHICS

It was the natural way of life that impressed Chuang Tzŭ. He saw man as originally happy but subsequently suffering through artificial changes because of his own efforts to modify nature and impose on others his own ideas. Chuang Tzŭ said:

Cherish that which is within you, and shut off that which is without; for much knowledge is a curse.

He named five causes of the impairment of original nature:

> The first is the five colors, which confuse the eye and thereby prevent its seeing clearly. The second is the five notes, which confuse the ear and thereby prevent its hearing distinctly. The third is the five odors, which penetrate the nose and dull its perception. The fourth is the five flavors, which cloy the taste and thereby disorder its acuteness. And the fifth is the likes and dislikes, which make the heart erratic. So original nature is dissipated. These are the five evils of life.

Chuang Tzŭ therefore counseled:

> Let there be absolute repose and absolute purity; do not weary your body, nor disturb your vitality—and you will live forever. For if the eye sees nothing and the ear hears nothing, then the soul will perceive the body, and the body will live forever.

What man does require is an understanding of the nature of things, that both life and death are merely part of the great process of reverse evolution like the succession of day and night and the change of the seasons.

Ideally man

> . . . knows not whence we come into life nor where we go in death—nor what to put first

and what last. He is ready to be transformed into other things without caring into what he may be transformed.

This ideal, suspended state is well illustrated in the following autobiographical statement by Chuang Tzŭ:

> Once upon a time, Chuang Chou [i.e., Chuang Tzŭ] dreamt that he was a butterfly, fluttering about—to all intents and purposes a butterfly. It did not know that it was Chuang Chou. Suddenly, he awoke, and there he was, Chuang Chou again. But he did not know whether he was Chuang Chou, dreaming he was a butterfly, or whether he was a butterfly dreaming he was Chuang Chou.

Chuang Tzŭ regarded the fear of death as one of the principle sources of human unhappiness. However, through the understanding he preached, this fear would become meaningless. The story of Chuang Tzŭ and the skull is well worth recalling in this connection:

> On his way to Ch'u, Chuang saw a skull by the roadside. Striking it with his riding whip, he bent over it and asked:
> "Sir, was it some insatiable ambition and inordinate desire that brought you to this? The fall of a kingdom that made you perish by the axe and halberd? Or had you lived an evil life and left a blot on the family name, and so were brought to this? Was it hunger and cold that did

this, or was it that you were brought to this by the natural course of old age?"

Then he picked the skull up, and placing it under his head as a pillow went to sleep. At midnight, the skull appeared to him in a dream and told him of the happiness of the dead. Chuang Tzŭ, however, did not believe this, so he asked whether the skull would wish to be restored to life and sent back to his home.

At this the skull opened his eyes wide and furrowed his brows, saying: "How can you imagine that I would cast away happiness greater than that of a king only to go back again to the toils and troubles of the living world?"

The end result, the ideal of life, according to Chuang Tzŭ, was a state where a man

> ... will bury gold in the hillside and cast pearls into the sea. He will not struggle for wealth, nor for fame. He will not rejoice at long life, nor will he grieve over early death. He will not find pleasure in success, nor will he feel pain in failure. He will not account the throne of a state as his personal gain, nor will he claim the empire of the world as his personal glory. His glory is to have the insight that all are one and that life and death are the same.

This blissful ecstasy marked by no will, no consciousness, no knowledge—where a man becomes like a child who follows nature purely, and "moves without knowing whither, and stops without knowing why . . . not conscious of anything, but adapts himself to the natural conditions of existence . . ."—this was Chuang Tzǔ's ideal life, which he called "the Happy Excursion."

As we might expect from the preceding discussion, Chuang Tzǔ had absolutely no use for government. He argued that civilization is an artificial structure that serves only to inhibit man and to keep him from living according to his natural instincts. He maintained that the true society is the primitive one built on natural equality and the native integrity of humanity. Just as man becomes unhappy when he loses the natural, childlike state, so society went astray when it fettered men with ceremonies, moral restraints and social obligations.

However, Chuang Tzǔ placed the blame for the structure of civilization not on the people but upon the sages:

> When the sages appeared, they worried the people with ceremonies and music for rectifying their bodies. They tripped the people with human-heartedness and righteousness for satisfying their minds. Thereby, the people began to develop a taste for knowledge and to struggle one with the other in their desire for gain.

With the emergence of social institutions, Chuang Tzǔ concluded angrily that "gangsters appeared."

He compared the actions of the sages with those of

a Lu prince who killed a stray seabird with wine, meat and temple music. The tragedy, of course, was due to the prince's ignorance of the bird, which he treated like himself and not as a bird.

> Had the prince treated the bird as a bird, he would have let it roost in dense forests, wander over open land, swim in the river and lake, feed upon fish, fly and rest in peace.

Government is like the prince; the people like the bird. The people, too, will suffer if they are required to follow what others consider right and good for them. And like the bird, which cannot be tamed without some form of coercion, the people cannot be governed without force of some kind. Therefore, the very purpose of government must be coercion. Therefore, Chuang Tzŭ concluded emphatically, the ideal government is nongovernment.

In this ideal, Chuang Tzŭ followed his master, Lao Tzŭ, although for somewhat different reasons. The latter had focused on the principle that "reversion is the movement of *Tao*," and he had argued that the more one governs, the less one succeeds. The former, in his stress on the free development of man's nature, demanded that people be left alone.

[4]

VIEWS AND KNOWLEDGE

According to Chuang Tzŭ there are two levels of knowledge: that which is learned through our senses is known as the "lower level"; that which is reflected in our mind is known as the "higher level." Chuang Tzŭ bewailed the fact that man is easily contented with the former, thereby neglecting the latter.

The following story offers a good illustration of what Chuang Tzŭ meant by the lower level of knowledge:

> It was the time of autumn floods when all streams poured into the river so that it swelled and spread far and wide. . . . The spirit of the river was well pleased that all lovely things of the earth seemed to be gathered to him. Down with the stream he journeyed east, until he reached the ocean. There, he looked still further east and saw no end to the waters. Then he turned his head and said to the spirit of the ocean, with a deep sigh: "There is a proverb that a man who has heard but part of the *Tao* thinks none equal to himself. And such a man am I. Had I not reached your abode, I should have made myself a laughingstock."
>
> Upon which the spirit of the ocean replied:

"You cannot speak of ocean to a well frog; its sphere is limited. You cannot speak of ice to a summer insect; its capacity is restricted by time. You cannot speak of *Tao* to a pedagogue; his scope is confined by teachings. But now that you have emerged from your narrow sphere and have seen the great ocean, you know your own insignificance, and I can speak to you of great principles."

The spirit of the river, in his original and entirely limited knowledge, is comparable to a man who relies solely on the evidence of his senses. The problem is that one whose knowledge is thus restricted or, in the words of Chuang Tzŭ, "does not reach to the positive-negative domain," cannot understand the "great principles." For such knowledge consists simply of sense-impressions and therefore yields contradictions. Being thus limited and finite, it offers no objective standard of truth. So Chuang Tzŭ said: "That which I may know may not be known; that which I do not know may be known."

In Chapter 2, entitled "Chi Wu Lun" or "On the Equalization of Things," Chuang Tzŭ offered an elaborate discussion of knowledge. He maintained that knowledge in its usual meaning, being thus finite and limited in scope, is liable to dispute and capable of no conclusion. The fact that people dispute about anything implies that they believe in the existence of an objective truth. Since knowledge offers no objectivity, there is no way to determine which side is right or wrong. So Chuang Tzǔ said:

> Supposing I am arguing with you, and you get the better of me. Does the fact that you win and I lose imply that you are really right and I, wrong? Or if I get the better of you, does that imply that I am right and you, wrong? For that matter, must one of us necessarily be right and the other, wrong? Or may we not both be right or both wrong? Neither you nor I can know....

What seemed to Chuang Tzǔ to justify his argument concerning this lower level of knowledge was the fact that in such a world of perfectly natural change, all things are equal, and absolute truth and absolute good are unknowable. In the human world, concepts of right and wrong are built up by man on the basis of his one-sided view; thereby, "there is nothing which is not good, nothing which is not bad." All these views are relative. There is no way of knowing objectively what is right and what is wrong so long as man remains at the lower level.

The higher level of knowledge is the same as the "understanding" mentioned previously as requisite for man's identification with the universe and nature. As to this level, Chuang Tzǔ said:

> The knowledge of the ancients was perfect. How so? At first, they did not yet know that there

were things. This is the most perfect knowledge; nothing can be added. Next, they knew that there were things, but they did not yet make distinctions between them. Next they made distinctions, but they did not yet pass judgments on them. But when the judgments were passed, the Whole (*Tao*) was destroyed. With the destruction of the Whole, individual bias arose.

Knowledge belonging to the lower level, as just discussed, aimed at making distinctions between right and wrong, "this" and "that," life and death, the "me" and the "non-me." Therefore, to discard this lower knowledge is to forget these distinctions. Once all distinctions are forgotten, there remains only the One, which is the great Whole. This act of transcending distinctions constitutes the higher knowledge, what Chuang Tzŭ termed "knowledge that is not knowledge." This higher knowledge, accordingly, is knowledge learned by the physical senses; it is simply an inevitable, natural growth in which the purpose of man has no part.

It is said in the "Chi Wu Lun" (Chapter 2):

The "this" is also "that." The "that" is also "this." The "that" has a system of right and wrong. The "this" also has a system of right and wrong. Is there really a distinction between "that" and "this"? Or, in fact, is there none? That the "that" and the "this" cease to be opposites is the

> very essence of *Tao*. Only the essence, an axis as
> it were, is the center of the circle responding to
> the endless change. The right is an endless
> change; the wrong is also an endless change.

In other words, these opposites are like an endlessly revolving circle and thereby blend into an infinite One, the eternal and omnipresent *Tao*.

Furthermore, the essence of *Tao* is to see nothing, hear nothing and do nothing.

> Let your hearing stop, and let your mind stop. Let
> your spirit, however, be like a blank, passively
> responsive to externals. In such open receptivity
> only can *Tao* abide.

The final goal is the ecstasy of being absorbed into the Whole, in a state marked by repose, quietude, harmony and inaction. One cannot push his way into this ecstasy; it must come of itself, in utter spontaneity. This is what William James called the "felicity of the sensorial life," which is a consequence of the native disposition but not the result of the conscious will.

In the light of this ideal, all conscious human endeavors as suggested by the very existence of a social, civilized structure, appeared to Chuang Tzŭ not only foolish but—worst of all—harmful.

[5]

AN ESTIMATE

Chuang Tzǔ had three characteristics in common with his master, Lao Tzǔ. First, both philosophies consider human nature as good and the state of nature as the norm. They favor anarchistic individualism and revolt against artificial conventions and institutions. Hence, they teach the abolition of culture and the practice of nongovernment in order to return to the state of primitivity, as characterized by spontaneity and naturalness.

Second, their philosophies, while accepting a prime truth, hold this truth unattainable through intellectual procedures. Instead, a form of contemplation and inward illumination is necessary. Hence, instead of teaching such artificial virtues as human-heartedness and righteousness, they advocated the doctrine of *wu wei* or "inaction."

Third, with their talk of the unreality of the visible world and the need for conforming to the *Tao*, both enter into what is really mysticism.

There are also three points that serve to distinguish Chuang Tzǔ from Lao Tzǔ. First, their conceptions of *Tao* differ. According to the master, *Tao* is the unity of being and nonbeing. "All things in the universe arise out of being, and being out of nonbeing." Thus, the translation from nonbeing to being is involved, but in a recurring cycle. Lao Tzǔ concluded that being and nonbeing, therefore, involve each other. But according to Chuang Tzŭ, *Tao* is the unity of nonbeing, which is being; and being, which is nonbeing: "All things arise out of nonbeing, which is being, for being cannot arise out of itself as a being, but out of nonbeing, which is being." Thus, although there is a transition from nonbeing into being, it does not stop there: progress is made in a new age of existence, a new world. Therefore, instead of teaching the cyclical normalcy of *Tao* as held by Lao Tzŭ, Chuang Tzŭ advocated the "transformations of *Tao*."

Secondly, the two also differed in their ideas on the evolution of the universe. Lao Tzŭ emphasized the general principle that "reversion is the motion of *Tao*"; that is, if any movement goes to its extreme of development, it necessarily has to excute a return or reversion: "The hurricane never lasts the whole morning, nor the cloudburst, the entire day." This constitutes the invariable law of nature. Were the universe not to conform to this invariable law, it would cease to function. But Chuang Tzŭ held to the natural flow of spontaneity; this is the basis of his theory of returning to nature. So when we say *Tao* produces all things, we mean nothing more than the plain fact that all things produce themselves, naturally and spontaneously. The difference here is best seen in the reasons each of these philosophers had for desiring nongovernment.

Third and finally, they disagreed on the ideal life. Both taught that we should retreat from civilization to primitivity. According to Lao Tzŭ, this is the royal way to the achievement of an ideal society. Thus, although his simple life repudiated civilization, Lao

Tzŭ did not reject this world. But according to Chuang Tzŭ, retreat is the royal way to what he called "the Happy Excursion," something ideal beyond the real of any society. So he said: "The supreme man should station himself outside of Heaven and Earth and withdraw from all things, to where there is nothing to fetter the soul."

Yang Chu

"What are the things that make life worth living?
They are sensual gratifications, such as the
pleasure of food and dress and the enjoyment
of music and beauty."
Lieh Tzŭ, Ch. "Yang Chu."

5. Yang Chu

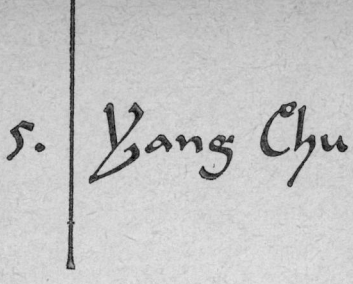

Yang Chu is remembered for his doctrine of self-love and sensual enjoyment. Although he is difficult to categorize in his philosophical assertions, he comes closest to Taoism because of his nonmoral conception of life and his fatalistic belief in death.

Apparently, the death of Lao Tzŭ led to a division of Taoism into two schools. The first was represented by Chuang Tzŭ who, as we have just seen, construed *Tao* as the totality of spontaneity of all things in the universe—leaving all things to follow their natural course. This school may be classified as naturalistic Taoism. The other school was that of Yang Chu. He saw *Tao* as a blind physical force that produced the world, not by design of will, but by necessity or chance. This view represents materialistic Taoism. Both views are recorded in the works of the legendary Taoist philosopher, Lieh Tzŭ.

[1]

LIFE AND WRITINGS

Only a few facts are known about Yang Chu's life. He was an inhabitant of the state of Chao (the modern province of Shansi). Chao was one of the three fragments of the state of Tsin, whose disintegration heralded the period of Warring States (480–222 B.C.), Yang Chu came of a very respectable family that could trace its origins to the royal house of Chou. His direct ancestor, the younger son of King Hsüan (827–781 B.C.), was the prince of Yang, a state soon to be absorbed by the state of Tsin. There is reason to suppose that Yang Chu had sufficient wealth for the leisure then essential for a life devoted to philosophy. It is also reasonably possible to place his life somewhere between the fifth and fourth centuries B.C. In Liu An's *Huai-Nan Tzŭ*, it is implied that he was younger than Mo Tzŭ (*c.* 468–*c.* 390 B.C.) and older than Mencius (*c.* 372—289 B.C.).

That which Mo Tzŭ had constructed was disclaimed by Yang Chu. That which Yang Chu had constructed was disclaimed by Mencius.

Our only source for his teachings is doubtful, one chapter in the above-mentioned Taoist book *Lieh Tzŭ*, but his basic ideas may be found in other Taoist works.

[2]

THE BASIS OF HIS TEACHING—FATALISM

Yang Chu's teaching, deducible from the doctrine of *wu wei* (nonaction), states that all that happens in the universe is predetermined by destiny. Life and death, success and failure, wealth and power, all are determined by destiny, in that free will, design or purpose—either of God or man—has no part. This fatalism provided a good excuse for self-indulgence in the world. In the *Lieh Tzǔ*, there is a chapter entitled "Effort and Destiny," that offers a good illustration of the meaning here:

Effort said to Destiny: "Your achievements are not equal to mine."

"Please tell me what you achieve," retorted Destiny, "that you would compare yourself to me?"

"Why," said Effort, "all life, success and wealth of man are under my control."

To this, Destiny replied, "Pêng Tzǔ's wisdom did not exceed that of Yao and Shun [two sage-kings of the legendary period]; yet, he lived to the age of eight hundred years. The ability of Yen Yüan [Confucius' favorite disciple] was not inferior to that of the average man; yet, he died at the age of thirty-two. The virtue of Confucius was not inferior to that of a prince; yet, he was embarrassed by hunger in the states of Chen and Tsai. The conduct of Chow [the wicked king of

Shang] was not superior to that of his ministers; yet, he reigned over the state.... If these results are encompassed by your effort, how is it that you allotted long life to Pêng Tzŭ and an untimely death to Yen Yüan—that you awarded discomfiture to the Sage and success to the impious; humiliation to the wise man and high honors to the fool, poverty to the good and wealth to the wicked?"

"If, as you say," rejoined Effort, "I have really no control over events, is it not then by your management that things turn out as they do?"

At this point, Destiny replied: "The very name Destiny shows that there can be no management. When the way is straight, I push on; when it is crooked, I let it be. Old age and early death, failure and success, high rank and humble position, riches and poverty—all these come naturally and of themselves. Of their ultimate causes, I am ignorant. How could it be otherwise?" *

All that happens in the universe is thus predetermined and beyond the control of human effort. What is necessary is to live in accord with one's destiny and thereby add zest to the enjoyment of life. Yang Chu's chief argument was based on his observation of the transitoriness of life:

One hundred years is the limit of a long life. Not one in a thousand ever attains to it.

---

* All extracts in this chapter are from the *Lieh Tzŭ*, unless otherwise noted.

And even if we do, Yang Chu contended, a large part of our life is spent in unconscious infancy and old age, long hours of sleep, pain and sickness, sorrow and fear. Consequently:

> There is not one hour free from some anxiety. What then is the purpose of life? What then is the happiness of life? It is in rich food and fine clothing and in music and beauty.

Hedonism is the outcome here. Since the world, as we know it, is a world of change and mutation, since fame and praise are ephemeral, the royal road to a happy life is that of sensual gratifications, such as the pleasures of food and dress and the enjoyment of music and beauty. Yang Chu concluded forcefully:

> The state in which all things differ is life; that in which all things are alike is death. During life, there are differences, as between intelligence and dullness, honor and meanness. But in death there is only the equality of rottenness and putrefaction. Neither can be prevented.... Some die at the age of ten; some, at one hundred. The wise and benevolent die as well as the cruel and imbecile. Therefore, let us hasten to enjoy life and pay no attention to death.

The best way for this enjoyment is

> ... to give it its free course, neither checking nor obstructing it.... Allow the ear to hear what

it likes, the eye to see what it likes, the nose to smell what it likes, the mouth to speak what it likes, the body to enjoy what it likes, and the mind to do what it likes.

The more desires that are satisfied, the more life is worth living. Hence, obstruction of desires is

> . . . the source of the most painful vexations. To check this source of obstruction and with calm enjoyment to await death for a day, a month or a year, is what is understood by enjoying life.

[3]

THE IDEAL OF LIFE—EGOISM

The ideal of egoism is the essence of Yang Chu's philosophy. It is based on two fundamental ideas: first, "each one for himself"; second, "the despising of things and the valuing of life." Some of the reasoning behind this ideal emerges in the following story:

> Ch'in Tzŭ asked Yang Chu: "If by plucking out a single hair of your body you could save the world, would you do it?"
> Yang Chu answered: "The world is not to be saved by a single hair."
> Ch'in Tzŭ said: "But supposing you could, would you do it?"
> When Yang Chu gave no answer, Ch'in Tzŭ

went and told Mêng-sun Yang, who replied: "You do not understand the mind of the Master. I will explain it. Supposing by tearing off a piece of your skin, you were to be rewarded ten thousand pieces of gold, would you do it?"

Ch'in Tzŭ said: "I would."

"Supposing by cutting off one of your limbs," Mêng-sun Yang again asked, "you were to be rewarded a kingdom, would you do it?"

Ch'in Tzŭ was silent.

Then, Mêng-sun Yang said: "A single hair is unimportant compared with skin, and a piece of skin is unimportant compared with a limb. However, many hairs put together are as important as a piece of skin, and many pieces of skin put together are as important as a limb. Therefore, a single hair is one of the ten thousand parts of the body. How can we disregard it?"

This egoism is tinged with Taoist thought. According to Yang Chu, the Great Universe is a large substance, and our ego is the small substance that arises out of the large. Our body is the form of the substance. Form cannot exist on its own account but is dependent on substance. Substance has reality in itself; it meant for Yang Chu that which has its whole being in itself, that is, the ego. Therefore, our forms are different, but our substances are the same. If all men are in accord with their differences in the hedonistic pursuit of pleasure, men will be satisfied and the world will be in peace and harmony. Hence, Yang Chu's principle of "each one for himself," positively stated, is: "One must mind one's own business." Negatively, the principle runs: "Do not meddle with others." This principle agrees with the whole rationale of Taoist thought.

In the same chapter "Yang Chu" in the *Lieh Tzŭ*, Yang Chu is reported to have said:

> The men of antiquity, if by injuring a single hair they could have profited the world, would not have done so. Had the world been offered to them as their exclusive possession, they would not have accepted it. As nobody would injure even a single hair and nobody would do a favor for the world, then the world would be in perfect order.

This provides an indication of the other aspect of his egoism—his principle of "despising things and valuing life." The reasons for this are suggested by the following passage:

> Man, living in the universe and possessing the nature of the five elements, is the most sagacious of all creatures. But his limbs cannot defend him; nor can his skin resist attacks; nor can his running avoid dangers. He has no hairs and feathers to withstand the cold and heat; he must rely on things for nutrition and his whole nature appeals not to force, but to reason. Reason is precious because it is developed out of man himself [literally "me myself"]. Force is worthless because it is imposed from the outside.

Similarly, "a single hair" is what is "developed out of me myself," and therefore it is precious. "The world" is what is "imposed from the outside," and therefore, worthless.

Moreover, Yang Chu argued:

> The people cannot live at ease because they long for four things: long life, fame, rank and wealth, which when achieved, render man afraid of ghosts, afraid of men, afraid of authority and afraid of punishment. Man then is in opposition to nature . . . and is governed by external conditions. But if he lives in accord with Destiny, he will not wish for [these things]. . . . He will be a man in accord with nature and governed by his internal self.

This attitude on Yang Chu's part was a natural by-product of his intense awareness of the world as a state of change and mutation. He reasoned that man could hope for little, worrying about the various transitory phases of the great cosmic life cycle.

Yang Chu's ideal attitude, even when faced with the greatest mystery, that of death, is evident in the following:

> Since there is life, let it pass and take its natural course. Then look for the satisfaction of desires and await the coming of death. Since death is near, let it pass and take its natural course. Then give rein to pleasure and make the most of

it. . . . Why should one mind whether it is early or late?

Sentiments such as these remind us of Epicurus, who said

> . . . the correct knowledge of the fact that death is no concern of ours makes the mortality of life pleasant to us, inasmuch as it sets forth no illimitable time, but relieves us of the longing for immortality. The most formidable of all evils, death, is nothing to us since when we exist, death is not present to us; and when death is present, we have no existence.[1]

Man, therefore, freed from the fear of death, has no worries save "to enjoy fully the beauties of this life and to exhaust all the pleasures of the present."

[4]

SOCIAL AND POLITICAL THOUGHT— INDIVIDUALISM

As a necessary corollary to his contention that man should take life as it comes, enduring and making the most of it and not bothering about others, Yang Chu maintained that there should be no moral code and social regulations binding the individual against

---

[1] Diogenes Laertius, *The Lives and Opinions of Eminent Philosophers*, translated by Younge, p. 469.

his own wishes. Since pleasure is the sole end of life, no moral law or social regulations externally imposed can invalidate its absolute claims. Nothing is wicked, nothing evil—provided it satisfies the individual's thirst for pleasure. Laws and regulations are the "obstruction of pleasure" and therefore the "source of the most painful vexation."

> Being warned and exhorted by punishments and rewards, urged forward and repelled by fame and laws, men are constantly rendered anxious. . . . Deliberating what they should hear, see, do and think, they lose immediate pleasure and cannot give way to sensual gratifications. How do they differ from chained criminals?

Yang Chu's ideal of the wise man was not the sage, but the man of the world, bent solely upon pleasure and restrained by no law, authority or custom; society would therefore only thwart wisdom. This idea of reverting to a state of primitive simplicity is pure Taoism; Yang Chu took it a step further in his requirement for gratifying our nature.

Obviously, the price of this extreme individualism and egocentricity is the destruction of the state, all established institutions, authority and conventions. This is, of course, too simple a way of solving the complex problems of the world. However, when we regard the trouble caused by people who seek domination and exploitation, Yang Chu's teachings of pure individualism are at least an intriguing temptation.

[5]

AN ESTIMATE

Pleasure was the entire foundation of Yang Chu's thinking. All else was merely an attempt to interpret the idea of pleasure. It is in the development of this doctrine that the defects of his system become apparent.

In the first place, Yang Chu maintained that pleasure must be positive, something produced by human efforts to satisfy human desires. One of the chief difficulties is that when there are desires there are also the conflicts of desires. Hence, we have to make a choice in order to satisfy desires. Yang Chu seems to have made the choice between the immediate pleasure and the remote pleasure, a choice between a physical and a mental pleasure. However, there are still difficulties. Even though, according to Yang Chu, we should prefer the immediate to the remote pleasure, the physical to the mental, yet there are still conflicts among the desires as well as among individuals. Yang Chu seemed to overlook this. He did not attempt to achieve a balance between men's desires and their satisfaction but simply demanded complete satisfaction. As a result, his ethical view ends in a rigorous and unbalanced anti-asceticism.

Next, Yang Chu wanted the pleasures that can be immediately realized but not those that can be achieved only with roundabout means. But pleasure, no matter how immediate it is, is an end in itself.

The means to the end may at certain times be deliberate and tiresome. Those who attempt to acquire some end without any sacrifice only deny themselves. This is exactly why the Epicureans had tried to modify the Cyrenaic doctrine, for they held that the sole end of life that can be realized is the absence of pain and the tranquillity of mind, which are themselves pleasures. Yang Chu by no means ignored the negative happiness of life, for he said:

> Enjoy life and take one's ease, for those who know how to enjoy life are not poor, and he that lives at ease requires no riches.

Despite this Epicurean spirit the trend of Yang Chu's argument for hedonism is that positive pleasure is more potent and intense than negative pleasure.

Yang Chu's ideal of happiness was not based on the return of the "lost paradise" nor on the assurance of immortality, but on the enjoyment of prosperity here and now. If this kind of life were realized, men would be in a state in which they would have no faith in the past, no hope in the future; they could only enjoy the present and await the coming of death. This may be a good state, but it is somewhat gloomy. As often happens with men whose ideal is pleasure, his view of the world was tinged with a gentle pessimism. This teaching was in sharp contrast to Confucius' moral endeavor and Mo Tzŭ's asceticism, which we shall study in the next chapter. Yang Chu's subtle pessimism, though, could not meet the insistent demands of the practical, everyday life.

Mo Tzŭ

"All-embracing love is the cause of the benefit of the world; mutual discrimination is the cause of its calamity."
Mo Tzŭ, Ch. 16.

6. Mo Tzŭ

In ancient times, the fame of Mo Tzŭ, or Mo Ti, founder of the school known as Mohism, was as great as that of Confucius. And his teachings were no less influential.

Unlike the other figures we have discussed, Mo Tzŭ came from the lowest class of society. His monumental contribution was that of an abstract principle of utility or utilitarianism, upon which he based ideas for a complete structure of society, state and religions. He disapproved of the elaborate rites of feudalism and taught a doctrine of all-embracing love. Each of these ideas brought down the wrath of the two existing schools.

[1]

LIFE AND WRITINGS

The life of Mo Tzŭ, like that of many of the ancients, is wrapped in obscurity. Even his name is a matter of uncertainty. The theory most commonly accepted is that Mo was not his family name. It is a name applied to a school of thought in the same way we apply the word "cynic" to the school of philosophy founded by Antisthenes. The original meaning of the word Mo was "tattoo," a form of punishment for slaves. Slaves in ancient times were either criminals or prisoners of war, who lived mainly in the cities in special quarters and were later trained to be artisans in certain trades. It is thus believed by many that the ancient Mohists were members of the artisan class with Mo Tzŭ himself a tattooed artisan. Likewise, Ti was not his personal name, for the word Ti might mean "a bird's feather" with which the tattooed philosopher decked himself in the manner of country folk. In any event, all available sources suggest that Mo Tzŭ came from a low stratum of society. This is the important fact to bear in mind in considering his philosophy.

We are not better informed about the dates of his birth and death. Roughly, he was born sometime between 480 and 465 B.C., and he died between 390 and 375 B.C. Although these dates are approximate, they establish Mo Tzŭ as subsequent to Confucius, contemporary with Yang Chu and older than Mencius.

As to his birthplace, there is strong and commonly accepted testimony that Mo Tzŭ, like Confucius and Mencius, was a native of the state of Lu. We know that he held a minor official position in the state of Sung and that he traveled extensively in the state of Ch'i and the state of Ch'u, where he probably died.

Very little is known of Mo Tzŭ's early life and education except that he studied under a Confucian scholar named Shih Chiu. Thus, we can assume his familiarity with the doctrines of Confucius and his acquaintance with Confucian followers among his own contemporaries. Assuming this, it appears that Mo Tzŭ in time became disappointed with Confucianism to the extent that he founded a school of his own. In the *Huai Nan Tzŭ*, a work of the second century B.C., we read:

> Mo Tzŭ had studied under Confucians and learned from them the doctrines of Confucius. But he soon found out that all the feudal rites were punctilious and vexatious, that the splendid funerals were extravagant, detrimental to the economy of the people and that the long periods of mourning detracted from the welfare of the people. Therefore, Mo Tzŭ abandoned the way of Chou and adopted that of Hsia.[1]

Though the teachings of Confucius and Mo Tzŭ were widely different, both men drew their inspiration from the sage-kings of antiquity. Just as Confucius had had the Duke of Chou as his idol, so Mo Tzŭ revered the great Yü, legendary founder of the Hsia dynasty (*c.* 2205–*c.* 1766 B.C.). It was Yü who successfully coped with a devastating flood, the Noachic Deluge.

> How grand the achievement of Yü! How far-reaching his glorious energy. But for Yü we should all have been fishes.[2]

---

[1] *Huai Nan Tzŭ*, Ch. 20.
[2] *Tso Chuan*, or *Tso's Commentary on the Spring and Autumn.*

Besides being the savior of the people, Yü was also noted for his self-sacrifice and devotion to duty. While he was combating the flood, he was so absorbed that he took little note of food or clothing and even thrice passed the door of his own house without looking in, though he heard in passing the wailing of his infant son. We also are told that Yü "bathed in the rain, combed his hair with the wind and rubbed his body smooth in the toils and privations of his traveling." [3]

The spirit of the great Yü was exactly the spirit of Mo Tzŭ who, coming from the lower levels of society, taught a philosophy of life ascetic in character and typical of his class. In fact, he not only preached but lived a life of rigid discipline and self-mortification. For the good of his fellow men, he and his disciples were ready to undergo any pain and suffering. It is for this chivalrous spirit of self-sacrifice that Mo Tzŭ, like his idol Yü, has been known to posterity as one who would wear his body smooth from head to foot for the sake of humanity.

Like Confucius, Mo Tzŭ was also concerned with the achievement of an ideal society and spent much of his life as a wanderer, seeking to publicize his great principles of all-embracing love and nonaggression. Also, while he was not the only one to see the harm of war, he was alone in taking definite steps to avert it. It was the offensive side of war that he blamed; its harmful effects could be nullified by a supremely

---

[3] *Chuang Tzŭ*, Ch. 33.

effective defense. Thus, he was not the idealist advocating mere good will or passive, unarmed resistance; his only hope lay in specialized defense forces and devices. As the Mohists came from the artisan class, they not only knew all the technical arts but also were eminent in practical military knowledge. For instance, Mo Tzŭ himself devised ingenious defensive measures against the scaling ladders, invented by Kung-shu Pan, the first Chinese architect and engineer, in a contemplated attack upon a city.

However, the most important aspect of Mo Tzŭ's teachings was its emphasis on the principle of utility and its religious appeal for his doctrine of all-embracing love. In carrying on his daily work, Mo Tzŭ undoubtedly regarded himself as engaged upon a mission in some way supernaturally imposed by the Heavenly Mind, and he thus founded the Mohist Society and remained at its head until his death. No fewer than three hundred enrolled in the Society, among whom one hundred and eighty were termed his faithful disciples, whom "he could order to enter fire or tread on sword blades, and whom even death would not cause to turn on their heels."[4] It was somewhat like a religious order, a strictly disciplined organization. Its essential ethics were that all members should "enjoy equally and suffer equally." Mo Tzŭ took this group concept as a basis and elaborated it by preaching the doctrine that "everyone in the world should love everyone else equally and without discrimination."

---

[4] *Huai Nan Tzŭ*, Ch. 20.

The same spirit and discipline were maintained after the death of Mo Tzŭ under the leadership of a Grand Master, elected from among the faithful. In this way, the Mo school also flourished during the period of the Warring States (480–222 B.C.) and did not really begin to decay until the first century B.C. However, the Mohists apparently did divide into three branches. In the *Chuang Tzŭ*, we read:

> There were disciples of Siang Li Ch'in, followers of Wu Hou, and Southern Mohists, including K'u Hao, Chi Ch'ih and Têng Ling. They all studied Mohism, but they held different views. Each of the rivals claimed its teachings as the true Mohism and accused others of being heretical. . . . Each of the rivals regarded its Grand Master as a sage and ascribed its tenets to him. . . . It is difficult to point with certainty to the one who was really the exponent of the genuine Mohism.[5]

The philosophical reflections of Mo Tzŭ are preserved in a book bearing his name. To be sure, a large part of the book is attributed to his disciples and followers. The work originally consisted of seventy-two chapters, but the modern edition has only fifty-three, among which three are undoubtedly spurious. His style is noted for its brevity and simplicity and for his use of colloquial expressions that are in great

---

[5] *Chuang Tzŭ*, Ch. 33.

part unintelligible. His obscurity was intentional, however. In the *Han Fei Tzŭ* we read:

> The Prince of Ch'u said to Tien Chiu [Mo Tzŭ's disciple]: "The system of Mo Ti is a notable learning. . . . Why are its expressions, for the most part, so unintelligible?"
>
> Upon which, Tien Chiu replied: " . . . the Master will elaborate and explain his thought in discussion, lest the reader should appreciate its literary style and neglect its practical application."

[2]

THE BACKGROUND AND SOURCES OF MOHISM

The teachings of Mo Tzŭ were intimately connected to the political, social and moral events of the time. The philosopher lived in the blood and turmoil of the Age of Warring States. Kings of the Imperial House of Chou were still nominal heads, but their real authority extended over only a small part of the empire. Each state had its own ruling prince or king, who threw off the semblance of subjection and pursued the objects of private ambition. With the decay of a central authority and with the disintegration of feudalism, there were no laws, no moral obligations and no social order. While the great states fought for prestige and power, the lesser ones struggled for safety and existence. It was to defend the weak against the strong that Mo Tzŭ and his followers devised the tactics of fighting a defensive war and techniques for building instruments for defending city walls. It was also to rectify this chaotic state of affairs that Mo Tzŭ enunciated his principles of all-embracing love and nonaggression. His program was one that could be counted upon to prove attractive to the war-weary people who wanted not so much social amenities, such as rites and music, as food, clothing and peace. This down-to-earth, practical approach is the essence of Mo Tzŭ's social and political thought; it is at the heart of his differences with Confucius and Lao Tzŭ.

To clarify this approach and the reasons for these differences, it is necessary to understand a lower-class background in Mo Tzŭ's day. Under Chou feudalism, the gap between nobles and commoners was great. The nobles, including aristocrats and the *shih* or educated bourgeoisie towered above the common people and were supported by them. They were the scholars, statesmen and diplomats while the commoners were nothing more than farmers born to the soil, on which they worked with no hope of advancement. In the *Mêng Tzŭ*, this social structure is outlined clearly:

> . . . There is the saying, "Some labor with their minds, and some labor with their strength. Those who labor with their minds govern others; those who labor with their strength are governed by others. Those who are governed by others support

them; those who govern others are supported by them." This is a principle universally recognized.[6]

As an innately brilliant and determined member of the oppressed class, Mo Tzŭ raised his outcry against such class distinction by advocating social equality and social utility.

In addition, like Lao Tzŭ, he opposed all the feudal rites and refinements of life so dear to Confucius—but for different reasons. Lao Tzŭ criticized traditional institutions and ceremonies as detrimental to the free display of man's true self. But to the proletarian philosopher, social amenities like rites and music were luxuries with no practical utility and harmful to the economy of the people, whose sweat and blood supported nobles abandoned to luxury and sensual indulgence. Nor had Mo Tzŭ any love for the Taoist "state of nature," in which, as he maintained, there could be nothing but disorder and chaos. Mo Tzŭ asserted complete justification for social institutions.

As we might expect, all the revolutionary views presented above brought down on Mo Tzŭ the wrath of the traditional schools. They accused him of sacrificing culture and the things that make life pleasant for bare economic benefit. But Mo Tzŭ anticipated these criticisms and found justification for his doctrines in the sanctions of Heaven. In short, he ended up using religion as a motivating force for his essentially utilitarian doctrine.

---

[6] *Mêng Tzŭ*, III, 1, 4.

[3]

ALTRUISM

Mo Tzǔ's chief interest was an ideal society. According to him, this society would depend on the principle of "loving one another" and "seeking one another's welfare." "Loving one another" is the theoretical basis of his idea; while "seeking one another's welfare" is the pragmatic. Mo Tzǔ made altruism the root of all the virtues, and he declared equal and universal love to be a duty. This is the core of his philosophy.

When conceived in this way, love is broader in scope and application than that which emerges from the human-heartedness of Confucius. According to the latter, love manifests itself in different degrees of intensity, so that there are various degrees such as filial piety, fraternal love and conjugal affection. But Mo Tzǔ insisted that love should be alike for everybody. This all-embracing concept, he contended, was the only panacea for the strife-torn world of his time.

In the *Mo Tzǔ* there are three chapters devoted to the subject of all-embracing love. He initiated the discussion by enumerating the great harms of the world:

> . . . attacks on small states by large ones, inroads on small families by large ones, plunders of

the weak by the strong, oppression of the few by the many, deception of the simple by the cunning and disdain toward the humble by the honored—these are the harms of the world.*

Then Mo Tzŭ pointed out the distinction between what he called the principles of "discrimination" and "all-embracingness." Under the principle of discrimination:

> ... the son loves himself, not his father; and so he injures his father for his own benefit. The junior loves himself, not his senior; and so he injures his senior for his own benefit. The minister loves himself, not the prince; and so he injures the prince for his own benefit. ... Hence, the father has no parental love for the son; the senior, no fraternal affection for the junior; the prince, no kind feeling for the minister. ... All these arise from the principle of discrimination.

But under the principle of all-embracingness:

> ... one is as much for other states as for his own; one is as much for other families as for his own; one is as much for other persons as for his own. Therefore, if the princes love one another, there will be no war. If the ministers love one another, there will be no riot. If men love one

---

* All extracts in this chapter are from the *Mo Tzŭ*, unless otherwise noted.

another, there will be no plunder. . . . Consequently, there will be no harm in the world, for all men will love one another.

Mo Tzŭ then concluded that the principle of all-embracing love should be the universal standard of action. Were everyone in the world to act according to this standard:

> . . . attentive ears and keen eyes would respond to serve one another, limbs would be strengthened to work for one another and those who know the proper principles would untiringly instruct others. Thus, the aged and widowers would have support and nourishment with which to round out their years, and the young and weak and orphans would have a place of support in which to grow up.

In brief, this was Mo Tzŭ's ideal human society, created only through the practice of all-embracing love.

The principle of nonaggression was developed out of the principle of all-embracing love. According to Mo Tzŭ, the two are closely associated. One who loves others must advocate nonaggression. And conversely, one who advocates nonaggression must love others. Mo Tzŭ devoted three chapters of his book to elaborating and illustrating this principle. In the first of these chapters, he offered a good illustration:

> Supposing a man steals peaches and plums from

another's garden. He is certainly condemned by the public and punished by the authorities. This is because he does harm to others for his own benefit. Next, supposing a man plunders another of his poultry and pigs; he is more unrighteous than the one who steals peaches and plums. This is because he does more harm to others. Just as he is more unrighteous, his crime is more serious. Then, supposing a man trespasses on another's stable and robs him of his horse and ox; he is still more unrighteous than the one who plunders another of his poultry and pigs.... And again, supposing a man murders an innocent person, tears off his clothing and takes away his sword; he is even more unrighteous than the one who robs another of his horse and ox.... All these are roundly condemned by the Superior Man as detracting from righteousness. Now the princes make attacks on other states, but they are not condemned and instead even praised for acting in conformity with righteousness. How can it be said then that there is any distinction between righteousness and unrighteousness? . . . Thus, supposing a man seldom sees black color; he knows well that it is black. But when he is used to seeing black, he will call it white. Again, supposing a man seldom tastes what is bitter; he knows well what is bitter. But a man who is accustomed to tasting [what is] bitter will call it sweet. And by the same reasoning, we condemn minor wrongs of individuals, but we praise offensive wars of the states as in conformity with righteousness. How can it be said that we distinguish between righteousness and unrighteousness? But the Superior Man must make the distinction.

As already suggested, Mo Tzŭ was not alone in his desire to abolish war. In an age of internal as well as external strife, many minds turned to this problem. For instance, a conference for the condemnation of war was held in 551 B.C. Later on, a proposal was made to divide the world into two "spheres of influence": one in the east under the overlordship of Ch'i; and the other in the west, under that of Ch'in. However, these were largely political tactics. It remained for Mo Tzŭ to take definite and positive steps. He did more than preach and theorize, for he and his followers prepared to defend the victims of war. One story has it that Mo Tzŭ, hearing that the great state of Ch'u was about to attack Sung, walked ten days and nights to Ch'u to dissuade its prince from his warlike purpose. At the same time, Mo Tzŭ posted 300 of his veteran disciples, armed with the implements of defense he had devised, on the city walls of Sung awaiting the invader's army.

[4]

UTILITARIANISM

Underlying Mo Tzŭ's entire way of thinking was his concept of utility, which led him to advocate benefit and harm as standards for judging right and wrong, good and evil. He said:

Benefit is what we are pleased to have. Harm is what we dislike to have.

These two words require further definition. According to Mo Tzŭ, what produces more good than evil is benefit and what more evil than good is harm. He said:

> To cut off the finger in order to save the arm is to take the greatest of the benefits and the smallest of the harms. To take the smallest of the harms is not to take the harm, but to take the benefit.

The point is that we must often forego a benefit if it leads in the end to a greater harm, and that we must be ready to undergo harm if it leads in the end to a greater benefit.

And again, in Mo Tzŭ's opinion, what is beneficial to the greatest number of people is benefit and what is beneficial to the smallest number of people is harm. For instance:

> ... a medicine that cures four or five persons out of ten thousand cannot be called a practical medicine.

Similarly:

> ... though four or five nations have been benefited by war, yet war cannot be made a practical policy.

On the other hand:

> ... if a man kills himself for the sake of the world, his suicide is beneficial.

This is in fact what Jeremy Bentham much later called the "greatest good of the greatest number."

For resolving the incompatible conflicts between benefit and harm, Mo Tzŭ maintained:

> We take the greatest of the benefits ... and ... the smallest of the harms.

In order to do so, there must be external and objective standards for judging benefit and harm beyond what we have just mentioned. So he said:

> For testing an argument there are three standards: ... to trace it, to examine it and to use it. Where to trace it? Trace it in the authority of the ancient sage-kings. Where to examine it? Examine it in the facts which the common people can see and hear. Where to use it? Put it into practice and see whether it is beneficial to the country and the people.

In fact, these three standards represent three methods of study: the historical, the experimental and the pragmatic. The historical method consists of taking the authority of the past as the basis for a principle; the experimental method is the investigation and verification of facts of the present; and the pragmatic is the foreseeing of future consequences.

Of the three, however, the most important is the third or pragmatic. According to Mo Tzŭ, that which is useful and beneficial is right and valuable; in other words, that which is of no use and harmful is wrong and of no value. Thus, Mo Tzŭ evaluated everything on the basis of its utility for the benefit of the country and the people.

> I asked the Confucians wherefore they should have music, and they answered: "Music is amusement."
>
> I said to them: "You have not answered my question. If I asked you why you should build a house, and you said it was built for protection against cold in winter and heat in summer and for the separate dwelling of persons of different sexes, you would then tell me why you built the house. Now I asked why you should have music and you said music is amusement. That is equivalent to saying that a house is to be a house."

In summary:

> The doctrine that can be put into practice is to be honored. That which cannot be put into practice is but a group of words.

But the question persists: What is it that benefits the country and the people? According to Mo Tzŭ, the answer involves wealth and population; and it is the increase of these two things that is at the heart of good government. As to the increase of wealth, Mo Tzŭ said:

> When a sage-king governs a country, the wealth of the country can be doubled. It is doubled not at the expense of others, but by utilizing the country and by cutting off useless expenditures.

"Utilizing the country" means production; "cutting off useless expenditures" means economy. Thus, production and economy are essential to the increase of wealth.

As to the increase of population, Mo Tzŭ said:

> It is the population that is not easy to double. But there is a way to do this. The sage-king had a law providing: "When a boy is twenty years old, he must have a home. When a girl is fifteen years old, she must have her man." . . . If we make a law that all should marry early, how can the population fail to double?

By Confucian standards, the average age for boys at marriage was thirty and for girls, twenty years. Mo Tzŭ held that if the people married ten years earlier than the age fixed by Confucius, then

> . . . on the average, one couple would produce one child every three years. Three children would be born within the ten-year period.

Thus identifying the increase of wealth and population with the greatest benefit of the country and the people, Mo Tzŭ went on to fight against luxuries, extravagant funerals, long periods of mourning and all other feudal rites and music that took place at the expense of wealth, which should be used for the food and clothing of the people. Attacking the lavish burials of his time, Mo Tzŭ wrote:

> Even when an ordinary person dies, the expenses of the funeral are such as to reduce the family almost to beggary. But when a ruler dies, by the time enough gold and jade, pearls and precious stones have been found to lay by the body, wrappings of fine stuff to bind round it, chariots and horses to inter with it and an immense quantity of tripods and drums, jars and bowls, halberds, swords, screens, banners and objects in ivory and leather to bury in the tomb, the treasuries of the state are completely exhausted.

Such observance of ritual and tradition at the expense of the country's prosperity was, in Mo Tzŭ's opinion, one of the greatest of evils.

[5]

RELIGIOUS THOUGHT

Three chapters of Mo Tzŭ's book are devoted to illustrating the will of Heaven, describing the existence of ghosts and spirits and denouncing the theory of determinism. These three points constitute the essence of his religious thought. The teachings of Mo Tzŭ, which originated from the people, were also intended for them. To the masses, what more powerful appeal could there be—particularly at an unhappy period of history—than that of the great deity, watching eternally over human affairs? Recognizing this and the need for a firm psychological basis for his principle of all-embracing love, Mo Tzŭ asserted that his theory was in accord with the will of Heaven. He thus conceived Heaven as the Sovereign on High (*Shang Ti*), who loves mankind and whose will is that all men should love one another. Mo Tzŭ further argued:

> But how can we know that Heaven loves the people? We know that because He enlightens them all. How do we know that He enlightens them all? We know that because He has them all. How do we know that He has them all? We know that because He receives sacrifices from them all. . . . All people are subjects of Heaven; why does He not love them all? Because one who kills the innocent will be punished by calamities. Who kills the innocent? Man. Who imposes calamities? Heaven. If Heaven does not love the people, why does He punish the unjust with calamities? Therefore, I know that Heaven loves all the people of the world.

Granted, this is not wholly satisfactory evidence for the existence of Heaven. But the point to remember is that Mo Tzŭ did not believe that men by nature love one another. He used religion as a motivating force for his great doctrine of all-embracing love. There are chapters on "The Will of Heaven" where Mo Tzŭ said little or nothing about the immortality of the soul or the "happy land of God." This is because his chief concern was the welfare of the living and the achievement of an ideal society. In this practical respect, his teachings, like those of Confucius, are essentially human and this-worldly.

Mo Tzŭ severely condemned his contemporaries for scepticism with regard to the spirit-worship that the ancient sage-kings practiced. In his chapters entitled "Proof of the Existence of Spirits," he spoke of spirits who have the same function of rewarding good and punishing bad as Heaven.

> Since the sage-kings of the last three dynasties died, there has been no justice in the world but brute force. . . . The world is in disorder. And what is the cause of this? The people do not believe in the existence of spirits, nor do they know that the spirits reward the good and punish the bad.

Mo Tzŭ cited a variety of examples to prove the existence of spirits. All the examples, however, contain so many superstitious elements that they are not reliable. But Mo Tzŭ, as a pragmatist, had no interest in pure metaphysical truth. His religious belief, as already noted, was mainly utilitarian: man's belief that spirits reward those who practice all-embracing love and punish those who practice "discrimination" afforded great incentive for accepting his doctrine. The following passage is illuminating in this connection:

> When Mo Tzŭ was sick, Tieh Pi [his disciple] came to see him and asked: "Master, you teach that the spirits are intelligent and can reward the good and punish the evil. Now, you are a sage. How then can you be sick? Is it that your teaching is not entirely correct or that the spirits are, after all, not intelligent?"
>
> Mo Tzŭ replied: "Though I am sick, it does not follow that the spirits are not intelligent. There are many ways by which one can be sick. Some become sick on account of the cold weather; some, on account of overwork. This is analogous to a house which has one hundred doors. If one door is closed, will there be no way by which robbers can enter?"

In the book of Mo Tzŭ, the doctrine of a providential retribution is given. As we have seen, Mo Tzŭ advocated this doctrine without special reference to hopes or fears connected with a belief in a life to come. With his utilitarian outlook, he denounced determinism, maintaining that men could perfect themselves by their own efforts. In this respect, it is interesting to note the different interpretations of destiny presented by Lao Tzŭ, Confucius and Mo Tzŭ. In Taoist writings, destiny is often used interchangeably with nature. Lao Tzŭ said:

... things are eternally shifting and restless; yet each is reverting to its origin. Reversion to the original means quietude. The state of quietude is the fulfillment of destiny.[7]

According to Lao Tzŭ, destiny means the existent conditions of the whole universe: that is, "being-for-itself." All things are the same in their fall and rise, in the growth and decay, but above all in the derivation of their being from their original nonbeing and their return to nonbeing. All this is the way of nature and is also the destiny of all things.

Confucius interpreted destiny in two different ways. First, it meant the will of Heaven or decree of Heaven. Confucius said:

If my principles are to prevail in the world, it is destiny. If they are to fall to the ground, it is also destiny [*ming*].[8]

He tried his best, but left success or failure to the will of Heaven. Second, he conceived destiny as something coming naturally and of itself, independent of effort. Hence, it is mainly important "to know destiny." Confucius said:

At the age of fifty-four, I know destiny.[9]

---
[7] *Tao Tê Ching*, XVI, 32.
[8] *Analects*, XIV, 38.
[9] *Ibid.*, II, 4.

And:

> He who does not know destiny cannot be a superior man. [10]

Adopting an opposing view, Mo Tzŭ denied destiny and devoted three chapters of his book to this denial. His argument may be summarized as follows. First, the theory of destiny is not in accord with the authority of the past. Mo Tzŭ said:

> In the ancient time, what was deranged by Chieh [the last king of the Hsia dynasty] had been put into order by T'ang [the founder of the Shang dynasty]; what was deranged by Chow [the last king of the Shang dynasty] had been put into order by King Wu [the founder of the Chou dynasty]. All in the universe stands unchanged, and the people remain the same. In the time of Chieh and Chow, the world was thrown in great confusion; but in the time of T'ang and Wu, the world was kept in peace. How can it be said that there is destiny?

Next, the idea of destiny is not in agreement with experience of the present.

> Whether there is destiny is a question to be decided by the senses of our eyes and ears. If our eyes can see it and our ears can hear it, there is destiny. On the other hand, if our eyes cannot see

---
[10] *Ibid.*, XX, 2.

it and our ears cannot hear it, there is no destiny. So far as our experiences are concerned, have we ever seen the object known as destiny and heard its voice?

And again, the theory of destiny is not in conformity with the consequences of the future.

If the sovereigns believed in destiny, they would be neglectful of their governments. Then the ministers would be neglectful of their official duties; men, of their plowing and farming; women, of their weaving and spinning. . . . As a result, the world would be thrown into confusion . . . and the people would suffer from lack of clothing and food.

From all this, Mo Tzŭ concluded that there is no destiny. He emphasized that if all that happens in the universe is predestined, men need not be afraid of the penalty of vice, nor need they care for the rewards of virtue. However, anxiety about the future is certainly one of the reasons for one to know destiny. So Mo Tzŭ suggested:

When we cannot reach a decision in our deliberation, we examine the past in order to know the future.

Doing this removes anxiety about the future. Without such anxiety, what reason is there for even trying to know destiny?

[6]

VIEWS ON POLITICS

The will of Heaven and the existence of spirits are examples of religious sanctions Mo Tzŭ employed to secure worldly peace and prosperity. In addition to religious sanction, however, political sanction is also needed—some form of organization and authority. In the *Mo Tzŭ*, there are three chapters on "Agreement with the Superior," in which Mo Tzŭ expounded his political philosophy. Strangely enough, Mo Tzŭ had a good deal in common with the political philosophy of Thomas Hobbes. Mo Tzŭ condemned the Taoist primitive society or what Hobbes called the "state of nature," in which there could be nothing but disorder and chaos.

> In the beginning of human life, when there was as yet no law and government, the custom was "everyone according to his own idea." Accordingly, each man had his own idea; two men had two different ideas; ten men, ten different ideas; the more men, the more ideas. Everyone considered his own idea as right and those of others as wrong. This set people against one another and led to hate and antagonism even between father and son. Discrimination and discord were rampant, with no harmony or unity. People killed one another with water, fire and poison. They would not

help each other. . . . The world was in great disorder. Men were like the birds and beasts.

But this "state of nature" soon became unbearable. No aggregation of people could long exist without some form of organization, of communication and of some degree of co-operation. Men then agreed to form political bodies and elected wise and able men to be their "emperors, ministers, princes and leaders," and to supervise the activities of the people, rewarding "all-embracing love" and punishing "discrimination."

The people understood that the cause of the disorder was the lack of a political ruler. Therefore, they selected the most wise and able man and established him as the Son of Heaven [emperor]. After the emperor was selected, they chose three wise and able men to be ministers. . . . Then they divided the world into a number of states and established princes for the various states. . . . Finally, they selected wise and able men to be their leaders.

Mo Tzŭ's state had a very prominent hierarchy. At the head of the body politic was the emperor, who was assisted by three ministers in charge of different phases of administration. Then, the realm was divided into various states governed by the princes who were in turn assisted by the leaders. The emperor, ministers, princes and leaders were all selected and established by the will of people in order to save themselves from anarchy. In this way, Mo Tzŭ viewed the state as the deliberate creation of man. How different was he from Confucius, who taught that "Heaven placed the people below and prepared for them the sovereigns and teachers!" Hence, if we call the political philosophy of Confucius "divine theory," that of Mo Tzŭ can aptly be regarded as the theory of "social contract."

Thus, before the existence of the state, there was great confusion and misery because too many ideas of right and wrong flourished. With its establishment, man surrendered his own ideas to the order of the sovereign, so as to secure peace of the world. Mo Tzŭ explained the necessity for this in the following passage:

> Now, in the state why is it that the superior cannot control the inferior, and the inferior do not obey the superior? . . . This is because there is no unity in the ideas of right and wrong. . . . If one is rewarded by the superior and at the same time discredited by the people, then the reward will not encourage him to do good. . . . If he is punished by the superior and at the same time praised by the people, then the punishment will not discourage him from doing bad. Therefore, I think that the cause of the fact that reward of the superior cannot encourage the good and that the punishment of the superior cannot discourage the bad is that there are too many ideas.

This resembles what Hobbes described as "the diseases of the commonwealth . . . that proceed from the poison of seditious doctrines; whereof one is, that every private man is judge of good and evil action."[11] This led Mo Tzŭ to his theory of the state, that is, the theory of "agreeing upward." His opinion touching this point is clear and simple:

> The heads of the families, in conformity with the order of the emperor, unify the ideas of their families and lead the people to agree upward with their leaders. Then the leaders lead their people to agree upward with the prince. And finally the princes again lead their people to agree upward with the emperor.

This was Mo Tzŭ's ideal state—one of complete uniformity. Hsün Tzŭ afterward criticized:

> Mo Tzŭ had vision in uniformity, but not in individuality.[12]

Since the state had been created to end the chaos resulting from conflicting ideas, Mo Tzŭ maintained that the state must be all-powerful, and the authority of its ruler absolute. Thus, the primary purpose of the state is "to unify the ideas," that is, to establish uniformity and suppress difference. In his theory of "agreeing upward," Mo Tzŭ emphasized:

> Upon hearing good or evil, one shall report it to one's superior. What the superior thinks to be

[11] *Leviathan*, Everyman's ed., p. 172.
[12] *Hsün Tzŭ*, Ch. 17.

right, all shall think to be right. What the superior
thinks to be wrong, all shall think to be wrong.

These ideas not only serve to characterize the Mohist
ideal, but they also reflect the political chaos and social confusion of the period of Warring States, which
caused the war-weary masses to cherish the centralized
authority advocated by their great proletarian philosopher.

[7]

AN ESTIMATE

In summary, Mo Tzŭ advocated a theory for the
organization of an ideal human society upon the principle of "loving one another and seeking one another's
benefit." He condemned aggressive war as contrary to
all-embracing love and set himself against costly funerals, elaborate ceremonies and even music, as detracting from the practical welfare of life. But Mo Tzŭ
fully recognized the weakness of man and hence con-
trived to embody the great doctrine of all-embracing
love in a Supreme Being in heaven and a monarchial
sovereign on earth. With the sanctions of punishment
and reward, both these authorities could induce the
people to conform to the "greatest benefit of the
world," which Mo Tzŭ maintained consists of wealth
and population.

If we are to form a just estimate of Mo Tzŭ's philosophy, we must get at a definition of the central
thesis of his system. The best way of doing this is by

juxtaposing the critical views of several modern Chinese scholars, who have contributed writings about the governing theory of Mo Tzŭ's philosophy.

Hsia Ts'êng-you, in his *History of China* (Vol. I) points out that Mo Tzŭ's fundamental thought is built on his religious belief:

> The belief in the existence of spirits has changed man's outlook. When this belief exists, man does not care much about life and death. He is ready to serve others and be sacrificed to others. Therefore, Mo Tzŭ was different from the Confucians, who esteem life above everything.

Liang Chi-ch'as, in his *A Study in the Works of Mo Tzŭ*, insisted that the central thesis of Mo Tzŭ's philosophy is the doctrine of all-embracing love.

> Mencius said: "Mo Tzŭ advocated the doctrine of all-embracing love, and he would willingly have worn his body from head to foot for the sake of humanity." Indeed, this statement contains, in germ, the whole teaching of Mo Tzŭ. His principle of nonaggression is developed from the doctrine of all-embracing love. Even his "Economy and Expenditure," "Simple Funerals" and his "Denial of Destiny" all flow from this one governing doctrine.

Hu Shih, in his *An Outline of the History of Chinese Philosophy*, maintains that the pragmatic method of Mo Tzŭ constitutes the essence of his philosophy.

According to him, the significance of Mo Tzŭ in the history of Chinese philosophy lies in his pragmatism, which he applied to all human actions as a standard of right and wrong and of good and evil. All else, such as all-embracing love, nonaggression, economy of expenditure or denial of destiny, is but "particular practice."

Hu P'o-an, in his *The Teachings of Mo Tzŭ*, advanced a somewhat different opinion that the system of Mo Tzŭ is based on the principle of nonaggression. He said that Mo Tzŭ lived in an age when China fell into great turmoil and misery and that thus the philosopher advocated this principle to secure the peace and prosperity of the world. Mo Tzŭ, accordingly, divided this great principle into two parts: one emphasizing its spiritual aspects—his all-embracing love, the theory of "agreeing upward" and the "will of Heaven"; and the other stressing its material aspects, which consists of his "economy of expenditure," "simple funerals" and "denial of destiny."

As a matter of fact, the significance of Mo Tzŭ in the history of Chinese philosophy lies in the fact that he produced an all-embracing system, which is difficult to define because of its ramifications in all departments of thought and reality. All the principles and theories that Mo Tzŭ developed mutually involve one another. For instance, his favorite doctrine of all-embracing love cannot exclude his principle of nonaggression. Similarily, his religious beliefs and political theory cannot be separated. The philosophy of Mo Tzŭ, therefore, is a systematic and coherent body of thought amid which, standing out as its central thesis, if there is any, must be his utilitarianism. This provides the touchstone by which all else is to be tested. But Mo Tzŭ must be remembered as having set forth not only this abstract principle of utility but also a complete structure of society, state and religion.

His significance in the over-all utilitarian philosophy is like that of Bentham—in his discovery of a method rather than a doctrine. But Mo Tzŭ's system may have been too utilitarian, as in its goal of setting up a uniform society on a utilitarian basis. In the *Hsün Tzŭ*, it is said:

> Mo Tzŭ was blinded by utility and did not know the value of culture.

Here, the word "culture" is used in the sense of "refinement."

In the *Chuang Tzŭ*, it is said:

> Man will sing, but he [Mo Tzŭ] condemns singing. Man will wail, but he condemns wailing. Man will express joy, but he condemns such expression. Is this truly in accordance with man's nature? . . . Contrary to his mind, man will not endure it. Though Mo Tzŭ himself might have been able to endure it, how is the aversion of the world to be overcome?

This was Chuang Tzŭ's prophecy of the failure of Mohism. The prophecy was fulfilled.

Hsün Tzŭ

"The nature of man is evil; his goodness is acquired."
Hsün Tzŭ, Ch. 23.

7. Hsün Tzŭ

Hsün Tzŭ was at the same time an exponent of the principles of Confucius and a critic of Mencius. If Mencius is taken as representing the idealistic wing of Confucianism, then Hsün Tzŭ may be said to represent the realistic wing because of his emphasis on social control and his insistence upon the weaknesses of human nature. We find that Hsün Tzŭ, though an energetic defender of the Confucian tradition, exalted the functions and prerogatives of the state, so warmly advocated by the Legalists, who scored their greatest victory in the reign of Shih Huang-ti (first emperor of the Ch'in Dynasty). Hsün Tzŭ's chief importance lies in the fact that he not only compressed the ideas of Confucius but absorbed the best thought of the other schools, such as the Taoist, the Legalist and even the Mohist, into his own teachings. In so doing, he summarized for posterity the intellectual achievements of the ancients in their most creative period.

[1]

LIFE AND WRITINGS

Hsün Tzŭ's personal name was K'uang, but he was also known under the name of Hsün Ch'ing. He was a native of Chao State, on the edges of Shansi, through which Hun, Turk and Mongol peoples entered China. His dates are not definitely known, but his working life fell mostly in the third century B.C. Like the other men we have studied, he was much concerned with good government, but he lived in an age when political and social turmoil was even more marked than in the time of Mencius. Mencius, as we have seen, proclaimed in more than one capital his great message that "the only foundation of national prosperity is human-heartedness and righteousness." But this great message failed to attract the attention of the feudal princes who were too busy pursuing the objects of private ambition. Hsün Tzŭ's time was like that, only worse. His teachings reflect the age.

Not much is known of the philosopher's life. In his early years, he was in Yen state. The king there was struck by Hsün Tzŭ's talents but hesitated to take him into his service. Then, Hsün Tzŭ devoted himself to academic research and teaching until the age of fifty, when he was invited to Ch'i state. Early in the third century B.C., Ch'i was eliminated as a major power, but its king, Siang, still opened his doors to wandering scholars. He honored Hsün Tzŭ with ceremony, valuing his teachings and applying to him for advice, and

Hsün Tzŭ appears to have taken part in politics for the first time. But the ministers and courtiers, in order to prevent his acquiring ascendancy in the court, felt it necessary to counteract his influence and spread scandals against him. Hsün Tzŭ threw up his post and then went to Ch'u state. Through the recommendation of Ch'un Sun-chun, the prime minister of Ch'u, Hsün Tzŭ was appointed the chief magistrate of Lan-ling. Like Confucius, he believed that a sovereign would win the allegiance of his enemy's people by his noble character rather than by powerful arms. Like Mencius, he held that a happy, contented, economically well-off population was the basis of good government. But the death of Ch'un Sun-chun led him to renounce his political life, although he never again left Ch'u.

In Lan-ling, Hsün Tzŭ surrounded himself with a group of young students, some of whom rose to eminence as scholars and politicians. For the remainder of his life, he devoted himself to this and to literary activity.

His manner of life was thus much like that of Confucius. Mourning over the degeneracy of his time, he entered on the vocation of social and political reformer. At first, he sought to effect his object by taking part in politics and setting an example of good government, as well as by instruction to young men. But he met with little success. However, Hsün Tzŭ remained an optimist, insisting that man would make himself master of his social destiny.

The teaching and personality of Confucius constituted the supreme intellectual impulse of his life and the inspiration of his entire thought. He said:

Confucius was human-hearted and wise; he was not blinded. Hence, he comprehended the *Tao* and was entitled to be ranked with the early kings.*

However, Hsün Tzŭ differed fundamentally from Mencius. He rejected Mencius' doctrine that human nature is innately good. He contended that, as an outgrowth of the extreme political and social decay, man by nature was evil. And in his conception of Heaven, Hsün Tzŭ leaned far over in the direction of the Taoists' impersonal, naturalistic *Tao*. He said that Heaven was no more than the unvarying law of nature.

> The stars make their rounds; the sun and moon alternately shine; the four seasons succeed one another; the *yin* and *yang* go through their mutations; wind and rain are widely distributed; all things require their harmony and have their lives.

Hsün Tzŭ was a superb educator. Among his disciples, the two most famous were Li Ssŭ, prime minister of the First Emperor of the Ch'in Dynasty, and Han Fei, a distinguished Legalist, both of whom stood for firm and authoritative government and for laws as the framework of social order. The results of their views are seen in the strong measures that consolidated the conquests of all-powerful Ch'in into an adminis-

---

* All extracts in this chapter are from the *Hsün Tzŭ*, unless otherwise noted.

trative and cultural whole. The doctrines of his disciples have led to the accusation by some Confucian scholars that Hsün Tzŭ, although classified with Confucianists, paved the way for the Legalist triumph, which culminated in the "burning of the books" in 213 B.C. Hsün Tzŭ died about 238 B.C.

The teachings of Hsün Tzŭ are preserved in a book bearing his name. The book originally consisted of three hundred and twenty-two articles, but after being edited and condensed, the number of the standard edition by Yang Ching of the T'ang dynasty is thirty-two.

For purposes of discussion, we shall view the system of Hsün Tzŭ under a fourfold division: human nature, desires, knowledge and politics. The theory of human nature includes the theory of education; for, as we shall see, Hsün Tzŭ was more interested in the educability of human nature than in its original constitution. The theory of desires affords the basis on which his whole system is built and includes therefore the institution of rites and music, which regulated man's mind and moderated his desires. The theory of knowledge deals with the nature of physical reality and sensible appearance and includes the theory of the mind, as well as the "rectification of names." Politics includes ethics and economics. In this latter combination, Hsün Tzŭ bore a marked resemblance to Aristotle; both speculated upon the purpose, nature and fortunes of the state.

[2]

THE THEORY OF HUMAN NATURE

Hsün Tzŭ denied divine authority and stressed human control. As to human nature, he denied supreme importance hereditary constitution and emphasized the role of acquired training. His definition of human nature is suggested in the following:

> Original nature, as conferred by Heaven, cannot be learned, nor can it be worked for. . . . That which, as brought about by man, can be either learned or worked for is acquired training.

Thus, original nature, as conferred by Heaven, is not a matter of human choice but an inevitable, natural growth in which the purpose of man has no part. But acquired training is the deliberate work of man in which our means can be adapted to desired ends. Hsün Tzŭ elaborated this definition further:

> Let us now consider human nature. What eyes can see and ears can hear is human nature. What can be seen depends on eyes; what can be heard depends on ears. Therefore, what eyes see and ears hear cannot be learned.

Elsewhere, Hsün Tzŭ said:

> Original nature is the unwrought material of the

original; what belongs to acquired training is the accomplishment and refinement brought about by culture. Without original nature, there would be nothing upon which to add acquired training. But, without acquired training, original nature could not become beautiful by itself.

Thus, human nature is a congenital quality of man capable of being improved.

According to Hsün Tzŭ, there are two kinds of mental activities: simple and complex. The simple consist, as above, of what the eyes see and the ears hear. These activities pertain to original nature. The others are complex and matters of human choice; they belong to the area of acquired training. Since complex activities originate in the simple, the simple can be combined to become the complex. For this reason, Hsün Tzŭ contended that human nature, as conferred by Heaven, can be improved through the effects of environment and experience so as to form refined personality.

Therefore, the sage improves original nature and gives rise to acquired training. When there is acquired training, there are rules of ritual and righteousness. When there are rules of ritual and righteousness, there are legal measures. All these social institutions are formulated by the sage. But the sage still resembles the multitude. He is alike to the multitude in his original nature; he is in contrast to them in his acquired training.

Thus, Hsün Tzŭ recognized individual differences and attributed them to the effects of environment and experience. He said,

> Although man is good and his mind discerns reasons, yet he must study under good teachers and associate with good friends. From good teachers, he hears the virtue of Yao, Shun, Yü and T'ang [four sage-kings of legendary times]. In good friends, he sees the conduct of loyalty, fidelity, honor and modesty. He is unconscious of the fact that he upholds in his heart human-heartedness and righteousness. If he associates with bad companions, what he hears are all kinds of evils, and what he sees are all sorts of lusts. Hence, he is unconscious of the fact that he inflicts capital penalty upon his person.

Hsün Tzŭ praised environment at the expense of original human nature. Whatever good the former achieves, it does so by triumphing over the latter. Hence, and in absolute opposition to Mencius, human nature is essentially evil. Virtue is the artificial result of training; vice, the spontaneous fruit of human nature. The following is the gist of his argument:

> Let us now consider human nature. By birth men possess the passion for profit. When they follow this passion, they strive to usurp all they can without regard for modesty and prudence. By birth men envy and hate. When they follow this passion, they seek the ruin of others without regard for

loyalty and fidelity. By birth men have the lusts of the ear and eye and a passion for music and beauty. When they follow these lusts, they commit excesses without regard for ritual and righteousness, culture and reason. Thus, when men give rein to their congenital nature and follow their feelings, they quarrel and grab, end up by opposing culture and confounding reason; and they culminate in violence. Only under the restraint of law and the influence of ritual and righteousness do men conform to modesty and reason and yield to order. From these premises it seems quite clear that by nature man is evil, and that if he is good, he is so because of acquired training.

But although man is capable of improvement, left to himself he will grow crooked.

Crooked wood needs to undergo steaming and bending; only then is it straight. Blunt metal needs to undergo grinding and whetting: only then is it sharp. The evil of human nature likewise needs to be rectified under the restraint of authority and laws and to be regulated under the observance of ritual and righteousness.

Hsün Tzŭ's reasoning was based on the theory that man was endowed at birth with intelligence and that this intelligence enabled him to transform the crude materials of his nature into a mature, refined personality through the process of cultivation.

> Every man on the street has the capacity of knowing human-heartedness and righteousness, obedience to laws and uprightness and the means for carrying out these principles. Thus it is evident that he can become a Yü [sage-king].

Whereas Mencius said that any man could become a Yao or Shun (sage-kings) because he is good by birth, Hsün Tzŭ argued that any man could achieve this same level because he is intelligent by birth. What man needs is to conform to the rules of ritual and righteousness.

[3]

THE THEORY OF DESIRE

While the central thesis of Hsün Tzŭ's system is his idea of human nature, the theory itself is based on desire. Hsün Tzŭ explained desire by saying:

> Man commences his life with desire.

And again:

> Desire need not be worked for, it is conferred by Heaven.

Since desire is the most natural and common aspect of human nature, it cannot be entirely eliminated—nor can it be easily satisfied. So he said:

Even though he be a gatekeeper, his desire cannot be eliminated: for desire is the fundamental element of human nature. Even though he be a sovereign, his desire cannot be completely satisfied.

Hsün Tzŭ was emphatic in believing that the prime cause of all evils is desire. But since desire is so natural and ingrained it cannot be eliminated. Hence, the secret of leading a virtuous life lies in the proper pursuance of desire through the functions of ritual, music and the mind. In other words, man's desire is to be regulated by ritual, to be moderated by music and to be rationalized by mind. The marked similarity here between the systems of Confucius and Hsün Tzŭ should be observed: ritual and music are prominent in both. The point where Hsün Tzŭ's thought diverges is in its emphasis upon the mind.

Man's desire must be regulated by ritual:

Whence does ritual arise? The answer is that man commences his life with desires. When these desires are not satisfied, he cannot remain without seeking for their satisfaction. When this seeking is without measure or limit, there is contention. When there is contention, there is disorder. When there is disorder, everything is finished. The early kings were disgusted with such disorder, so they instituted ritual and righteousness for the limitation of desires, and in order to cultivate man's desires and to guide his quest for things.

Briefly, ritual has three functions: to limit man's desires so that he need not strive to "usurp all"; second, to cultivate man's desires so that he need not seek "the ruin of others"; third, to hold desires and the things for satisfying desires in balance, so that there will be no strike. At this point Hsün Tzŭ emphasized:

> People desire and hate the same things. Their desires are many, but things are few. Since they are few, there will inevitably be strife.

Therefore, it is not only commendable but imperative to impose a limit on everyone in the satisfaction of his desires. The most important function of ritual is the setting of this limit, so that no one will commit excess nor will one wander from the path of duty and right.

Man's desires should be moderated by music:

> Music is an expression of joy, an irrepressible part of human emotion. Men cannot be without joy, and joy invariably breaks out in voice and finds expression in movement. . . . If this expression is not properly directed, riots invariably result. In view of this, the early kings invented the music of *Ya* and *Sung* [two divisions of the *Book of Poetry*], so that its sounds might express joy but excite no riot . . . and its composition and orchestration might inspire good thoughts and suppress evil notions.

In this way, music, together with ritual, is a powerful educative force that can stir up goodness in people's hearts and thereby keep them away from evil influences. Again, in Hsün Tzŭ's own words:

> Music, when performed in the ancestral temples, inspires the feeling of reverence among the sovereign and his ministers; when performed in the inner apartments, the feeling of affection among wives and husbands; when performed in the village squares, the feeling of amity among the multitude. Therefore, music unites to establish harmony, compares to enrich its notes and orchestrates to create beauty. While leading in one direction, it regulates the myriad of changes.

The difference between the functions of ritual and music is that where the former regulates man's desires and cultivates his outward conduct, the latter moderates man's desires and cultivates his inward sentiment. So Hsün Tzŭ said:

> Music is the constant harmony; ritual is the invariable propriety. Music establishes union and harmony; ritual maintains difference and distinction.

According to Hsün Tzŭ, all desires, if not subdued to reason, will lead to strife. What upholds reason is the mind, and hence the mind helps to guide man in the satisfaction of his desires.

> ... under the control of his mind, [man] is moderate in the satisfaction of his desires. ... When man's mind conforms to reason, there is order even though there are many desires. On the other hand, under the license of the mind, desires cause trouble if not satisfied. When man's mind acts against reason, there is disorder even though there are few desires.

And:

> The mind is the sovereign of the body and the master of the soul. It is the commander and not a receiver of commands. And therefore it is self-restrained, self-acting, self-disposed, self-contained and self-reliant.

Thus, the work of the mind is not merely to think but to deal with right or wrong in the moral sense. When the mind is motivated by reason, desires are subdued to humane purpose. But because the mind is often obscured by desires, Hsün Tzŭ held that mental purification is a prerequisite for the attainment of truth and goodness. At this point, Hsün Tzŭ made a suggestion that was to have great influence over a thousand years later on the Sung or Neo-Confucian philosophers.

[4]

THE THEORY OF KNOWLEDGE

At the outset, Hsün Tzŭ's distinction between sensible appearance and physical reality should be indicated. He held that only one "appearance" or form is real and that all others are mere illusions, i.e., mere appearance of the one that is reality. For instance, a stone bench, besides its original appearance of a bench, may appear like a tiger. A tree, besides its original appearance of a tree, may appear like a man. But the appearance of the tiger and the man are but illusions of the mind and hence they are not the real beings of things representing the physical realities of the stone bench and the tree. These sensible appearances do not flow from the stone bench and the tree; rather, they are reflected in the mind that has been beclouded by outward show and sham, hiding the real beings of things.

When a man is in doubt and absent of mind, he will not see external things clearly; for if our thought is not clear, we cannot decide between the real and illusory. While a man is at a distance, he sees a stone bench as a tiger and a tree as a man. For his sight is obscured. A drunkard crosses a deep gulf as if it were a narrow gap; he bends his body to pass the city gate as if it were a private chamber. For the wine confuses the mind. If a man closes his eyes and tries to see, he will take one for two; if he covers his ears and tries to hear, he will take silence for a clap of thunder. For the externals obscure his sense organs.

Thus, appearance is what is manifested in the phenomenal world; what is behind the phenomenal world is the realm of reality. Hence, reality is not visible to the senses but only discernible to the mind. There is a similarity between Hsün Tzŭ and Hegel in the fact that both held reality to exist at one level. Nevertheless, they gave different interpretations of this single level. For Hegel, the one level at which reality exists is the level of rationality, with the phenomenal world a mere reflection of the mind. In this, Hegel was metaphysically an idealist. But for Hsün Tzŭ, on the other hand, the level at which reality exists is the level of the physical world—reality has its self-existence and self-substantiality independent of mind. In this, Hsün Tzŭ might be called a realist.

> That in man by which he knows is called the faculty of knowing. That in the faculty of knowing which corresponds to external things is called knowledge.

The faculty of knowing consists of two parts: first, what Hsün Tzŭ called the "heavenly organs"—the senses of the ears and eyes; second, the mind itself. As to the function of the former:

> How and why can one discern similarities and differences? . . . through the "heavenly or-

gans..." The classification of different forms and colors is due to the sense of sight. The classification of sounds, tunes and voices is due to the sense of hearing.

Thus, the function of the "heavenly organs" is to receive impressions as produced by external things.

As to the function of the mind, Hsün Tzǔ said:

> The mind gives meaning to impressions.... The "heavenly organs" receive impressions and classify them, and only then can the mind give meaning to them. When the five organs note something but cannot classify it, and the mind tries to identify it but fails to give it meaning, then one can only say that there is no knowledge.

In other words, the mind perceives knowledge only after the "heavenly organs" accumulate the impressions produced by the external world. Hence, Hsün Tzǔ maintained that the capacity of the mind to perceive knowledge is not subjective or innate but acquired and enriched by experience. The common illustration is that when a child sees fire he touches it, because his mind at first does not perceive that fire will burn his fingers. After he has tried, his mind has this perception. In maintaining that human knowledge begins with sensations or experience as accumulated by the five senses Hsün Tzǔ can best be classified as an empiricist.

Moreover, as noted above, because the mind is often obscured by desires, mental purification is a prerequisite for the perception of knowledge. Once desires are subdued, the mind can become clear and then perceive knowledge, in the sense of truth. Hsün Tzŭ offered a good illustration of this point:

> Man's mind can be compared to water. When still, its dust drops to the bottom, and the water becomes clear on the surface. Only then can the realities of our figures be reflected in it. When a light, gentle wind passes over the water, the dirt is stirred up and beclouds the surface. As a result, the reality of things is not then reflected. So is the mind . . . if it is obscured by externals, it does not discern between falsity and truth.

The ultimate purpose of knowledge is to seek for the elaborate and noble *Tao*. Like the English "way," the Chinese *Tao* has the double meaning of a "road or pathway on which to go forward" as well as a "doctrine of truth, answering to the Greek *logos*." The idea of *Tao* is fundamental in ancient Chinese literature, both in the writings of the Confucian school and in those attributed to Lao Tzŭ and Chuang Tzŭ. The word *Tao* used by the latter is the "way of Nature," representing the noblest truth. Used by the Confucian scholars, it is the "way of humanity," the way in which human nature should unfold. For instance, in the *Chung Yung* or the *Doctrine of the Mean*, attributed to Tzŭ-ssŭ (492–431 B.C.), the grandson of Confucius, we read:

> That which Heaven confers is called Nature.

That which conforms to Nature is called the *Tao*.
That which cultivates the *Tao* is called Culture.

Although this general principle of the *Tao* was not peculiar to Hsün Tzŭ, his interpretation was unique. He agreed that the *Tao* is a single absolute truth, existing for all eternity and being transmitted in all things. But he maintained that most of the philosophical schools had seen only one aspect of the *Tao*, failing to know the whole truth. For instance:

Mo Tzŭ was blinded by utility to the neglect of culture ... Chuang Tzŭ was blinded by nature to the neglect of man. From the point of view of utility, the *Tao* is nothing more than seeking for profit. From the point of view of Nature, the *Tao* is nothing more than laissez faire. These different views are single aspects of the *Tao*. But the essence of the *Tao* is constant and included all things; it cannot be grasped by a single corner. Those who have partial knowledge perceive one aspect but fail to comprehend its totality. So they think it sufficient to gloss things over. Being confused themselves, they also mislead others. . . . This is indeed a great misfortune brought about by ignorance and blindness.

The term "the Rectification of Names" was originated by Confucius.

Let the prince be prince; the minister, minister; the father, father; and the son, son.

Every name should imply the essence of that class of things to which it applies. In other words, every name in the social relationships implies certain responsibilities and duties. Prince, minister, father and son are names of such social relationships, and the individuals having these names must fulfill responsibilities and duties accordingly. This application of "the Rectification of Names" theory was limited by Confucius to the principle of righteousness or—in the Western sense—to ethics. However, Hsün Tzŭ's theory was not so confined. It was closely associated with the principles of reason or, in Western terminology, the logical principles of theoretical knowledge.

As to the origin and purpose of names, Hsün Tzŭ said:

> Names were made in order to denominate actualities—on the one hand so as to distinguish the superior from the inferior, and on the other hand to discern similarities and differences.

Hence, names originated partly for social differentiation and partly for logical differentiation.

As to the logical use of names, Hsün Tzŭ further said:

> Names are given to things. Those which are identified are given the same names; those which are differentiated are given different names. Then, a simple name is given to what is simple; if the simple name is not applicable, a compound name is used. And again, if the simple name and the

compound name involve each other, a common name is used, for the common name does not give rise to difficulties. One who knows that different actualities have different names, and who therefore never refers to different actualities other than by different names, does not experience any confusion. Likewise, one who refers to the same actualities should not use any other but the same names. Moreover, although things are innumerable, they are denominated by one of two ways: sometimes we wish to generalize those which we call "things" (the term "things" is the Great General Name, which is so extensive and general that it includes all); sometimes we wish to specify those which we call "birds and beasts" (the term "birds and beasts" is the Great Specific Name which is so intensive and specific that it excludes all others).

From this passage, we can deduce the following conclusions:

1. Same names are given to those that are of the same kind, and different names to those that are of different kinds.
2. A simple name is given to what is simple, and a compound name to what is compound. For instance, "horse" is a simple name. If the horse is white, then a compound name—in this case, "white horse"—is applicable.
3. A common name is given to those that have a common characteristic, applying to both the simple and

compound name. For instance, "animal" is a common name for both "horse" and "white horse."

4. Great General Name is given to those that are denominated by the extension of "things." For instance, the term "things" is a great general name that includes "animals, plants and metals" and many similar items.

5. Great Specific Name is given to those that are denominated by the intention of things. For instance, the term "birds and beasts" is a great specific name, for birds excludes beasts and vice versa.

In view of the last two principles, it is evident that Hsün Tzŭ had a clear conception of the logical method for the denomination of things. The general name is the product of the synthetic process of reasoning, while the specific name is that of its analytic process.

Then, Hsün Tzŭ proceeded to the discussion of how a name is formed and what should be emphasized in the formation of a name.

> Name has no fixed standard. It is only by agreement that we apply a name. Once agreed, it becomes customary and the standard is thus fixed. That which does not conform to the agreement is opposed to the standard. Name has no fixed actuality; it is only a product of such agreement. . . . But name has its fixed goodness; that which is easily understood is a good name. There is a distinction between things which are similar in name and different in kind, and things which are different in name and similar in kind. Those

which are similar in name and different in kind, though they have the same name, are substantially distinct. Those which are different in name and similar in kind have a distinction which is but a transformation. Therefore, if there is transformation and no difference, the things must be one and the same.

[5]

ON POLITICS

Hsün Tzŭ was also interested in the problems of good government and maintained, as a necessary corollary to his theory of desires, that good government could be achieved by making evident the distinction between the superior and the inferior and the sovereign and the minister.

When no sovereign controls the minister; and no superior, the inferior, the world gives rein to desires. Desires are many; things, few. Since this is so, strife is then inevitable.

Hsün Tzŭ was consistent with his over-all theory in maintaining that the purpose of politics was to regulate men's desires, in order to keep them at their appointed station. He ended up advancing a theory that implies a demarcation of social classes.

Man has a common desire to be a sovereign and possess the wealth of the world. But this desire can hardly be complied with, nor can it be easily satisfied. Therefore, the early kings instituted rite and righteousness to delimit men's desires, in order to make demarcation of the superior and inferior, a distinction between senior and junior and a division between the learned and unlearned, and the competent and the incompetent.

Another passage explains this demarcation more fully:

Men cannot live without society. When there is no division [of social order], there is contention. When there is contention, there is disorder. When there is disorder, everything is finished. . . . In other words, division is a great benefit for man. The sovereign is the central authority for making this division. Hence, what he beautifies will beautify the fundamental of the world. What he pacifies will pacify the fundamental of the world. And what he honors will honor the fundamental of the world.

These divisions recognized two social levels. One stood for the higher group, including the "superior, senior, learned and competent," in general, all the upper strata. The other and lower consisted of the great mass of the "inferior, junior, unlearned and incompetent."

When the division is equal, there is no distinction. When the situation is equal, there is no unity. When the multitude is equal, there is no order.

When there are Heaven and Earth, there is a distinction between the high and low.

Hsün Tzŭ conceived a special position for the sovereign beyond that of central authority. He saw the sovereign as standing apart from all other men, not under a special commission from Heaven but under the general will of the people. In this regard, Hsün Tzŭ was in close conformity with the teachings of Mencius.

The sovereign is the source of a stream to the people. When the source is clear, the stream is clear. When the source is foul, the stream is foul.

And:

... the sovereign is like a plate. When it is round, its water is round. The sovereign is like a bowl. When it is square, its water is square.

In short, the sovereign is, first of all, an example for the people, a pattern for them to follow.

Still another passage explains the sovereign's position more fully:

... a sovereign is able to hold the people. How is he able to hold the people? It is the sovereign who is skilled in nourishing, governing, employing and protecting the people. One who is skilled in nourishing the people will be loved by them. One who is skilled in governing the people will be honored by them. One who is skilled in employing the people will be supported by them. One who is skilled in protecting the people will be glorified by them. The sovereign who possesses these four skills will certainly be supported by the world. This is why the sovereign is able to hold the people. On the other hand . . . the sovereign who is without these four skills will certainly be abandoned by the world.

The last sentence defined the general bias of Hsün Tzǔ's politics. Like Mencius, he supported the right of revolution against the sovereign who failed in the four ideal skills.

. . . the sovereign is like the boat; the people, like water. Water can carry the boat and at the same time overturn it.

In fact, these skills posed gigantic responsibilities for a sovereign. True, Hsün Tzǔ assigned him a unique and lofty position, but its real meaning was that of responsibility.

It should be noted that these ideas are in perfect accord with the modern theory that governments are instituted by the consent of the people, who have every right to alter or abolish government if it becomes destructive or harmful.

Stemming from Hsün Tzǔ's cynical view of man's original nature was his description of the primitive state as one of "beasts and birds," that is, "a state of strife." For this reason, he said it had been necessary to have teachers to guide and laws to correct man's evil nature. By means of education and legal measures the spirit of mutual courtesy is fostered, refinement of life cultivated and an ordered state of society established. This is why we have government and social institutions. However, Hsün Tzŭ remained true to the Confucian tradition in attaching the highest importance to the people and lesser weight to the sovereign. Thus, when he exalted the sovereign, he only meant to say that the sovereign possessed the way for attaining to good government.

> There is the Way; there is the state.
> When there is no Way, there is no state.

This way of a sovereign was outlined as follows:

> Employ those who are good and capable; promote those who are honest and respectful; encourage those who are filial and fraternal; support orphans and widows; and relieve the needy and destitute. When these measures are achieved, the people will be satisfied with the administration. When the people are satisfied, the sovereign will reign in peace and security.... Therefore, if the sovereign wants peace and security, he will love the people with fair administration, if he wants glory and honor, he will honor the scholars with ceremonies; and if he wants success and achievements, he will employ those who are good and capable. These are the great virtues of the sovereign.

The connection between private ethics and national politics is well set forth here; Hsün Tzŭ would have the sovereign govern his state by his noble character rather than by brute force. In fact, this system was not peculiar to Hsün Tzŭ, for both Confucius and Mencius had emphasized the good behavior of the ruler as a prerequisite for successful government. As we have seen, both absolutely discredited a despotic, high-handed rule and held that the man in power should himself be a pattern to those beneath him. Both of them quoted the saying: "The prince is the wind; the common people, the grass; and the grass bends in the direction of the wind." But Hsün Tzŭ, while recognizing the worth of virtue as an acquired goodness, and while expecting it, at the same time comprehended the evil nature of man. For this reason, in addition to the educative systems of rite and music, he said that man needed teachers to preserve his virtue and law to check his evil nature. Thus, although example is admirable and, in fact, essential, the restraints of law and moral influence are vital as well. Only under such restraints can man hope to overcome his true nature, which tends to violence and disorder.

Like Mencius, Hsün Tzŭ held that a happy, contented, economically well-off population is the basis of a good state.

> The way of enriching the state consists in the economy of expenditure, enrichment of the people and good management of surplus.

In his specific measures, Hsün Tzŭ aimed not only at reducing the heavy taxation on the people as a means of alleviating their desperate condition, but also at developing national resources for the increase of production. Moreover, he advocated the importance of agricultural education for improving productive skill and technique.

> Let the physiognomy of the land be surveyed; the character of the soil be studied; the five kinds of grains be tested; so agricultural operations may be improved and the crops properly preserved. When all these things are carried out in due course, the farmers will be industrious and satisfied.

The guarantee of the people's prosperity was only Hsün Tzŭ's first requirement for good government. Certain groups should be limited in number:

> When there are too many public officers, the state is reduced to poverty. When there are too many craftsmen and merchants, the state is reduced to poverty.

In another passage, advice is given as to the cultivation of the land and the breeding of stock:

> By proper nourishment, the six kinds of animals will prosper. By proper cultivation, grass and trees will flourish. And by proper administration, the people will form one unity. This is the system which was instituted by the sage-kings of the past and should be enforced by present wise rulers. ... Spring is the season for plowing; summer, the season for cultivating; autumn, the season for harvesting; and winter, the season for storing. If

the four seasons are not interfered with, there will be plenty of grain and corn and people will have an abundance of food. If rivers and lakes are carefully protected, there will be plenty of fish and turtles and people will have an abundance of these necessities. If cutting and planting are carried on at the proper time, the woods and forests will not be devastated and the people will have an abundance of timber.

[6]

AN ESTIMATE

In the work of building upon the foundations laid down by Confucius, Mencius and Hsün Tzŭ assumed the lead. Both revered the sage as their master and imitated him as a model. Both were chiefly interested in the problem of good government and stressed the economic basis of society. Notwithstanding these similarities, there are some points on which the two great philosophers differed fundamentally from each other. Their characters were different. Hsün Tzŭ was prudent, clear-minded and judicious, while Mencius was bitingly frank, high-minded and vehement. Their differences extended to their writings and their teachings as well. The writings of Mencius are eloquent in style and masterly in argument, while those of Hsün Tzŭ are elegant in style and more logical in argument.

Mencius believed that human nature is essentially good and therefore taught the practice of virtue as a necessary expression of that nature. From this premise, the cultivation of man's personality depends not upon the suppression of his outward conduct but upon the development of his inward mind. Accordingly, Mencius held that good government depends upon good administration, underscoring the need for moral cultivation on the part of the ruling class.

Hsün Tzŭ regarded human nature as basically bad and therefore argued for the proper training of this nature in goodness. He said that standards of action were needed that were to be found in the rules of propriety (rites). An important difference between the two men is obvious here. Whereas Mencius regarded rites as a mere outgrowth of the inner spirit of human-heartedness, Hsün Tzŭ considered rites as the most effective means of counteracting the inherent baseness of human nature. Indeed, Hsün Tzŭ laid the utmost importance on rites in morality. He claimed that rites not only provide the regulation for the satisfaction of man's desires but also give refinement and purification to man's emotions. Rites, when so conceived, denote something very important and basic in human life.

The age-old conflict between individual freedom and public welfare affords an insight into Hsün Tzŭ's achievement. Both Confucianists and Legalists (*see* Chapter 8) had strong but opposed beliefs in this area. Confucius and his followers maintained that people should be governed by rites and morality, not by law and punishment.

> If the people are guided by laws and all treated as equals in the matter of punishments, they may succeed in doing no wrong, but they will also lose

their sense of shame. On the other hand, if they are guided by morality and are treated as equals, they will reform themselves through a sense of shame.[1]

The Legalists stood for laws and for firm and autocratic government as the framework of social order. Hsün Tzŭ, however, seemed to reconcile these two views maintaining that law is documentary while rite is its essential practice. According to his teachings, laws cannot be well enforced if people do not behave in conformity with rite. Rites and laws are supplementary in keeping social order and cultivating personal virtues. Thus, Hsün Tzŭ attempted to build up a universal cultural pattern for the framework of human society.

Most important, where Confucius advocated *jen* or "human-heartedness" as the prime virtue of life and Mencius gave *yi* or "righteousness" the position of cardinal virtue parallel to that of *jen*, Hsün Tzŭ stressed *li* or "rites" as the principle virtue for upholding *jen* and practicing *yi*. Thus, *jen*, *yi* and *li* emerge as the three cardinal virtues that underlie Confucianism. They are the norms of conduct that have been followed by the Chinese people for thousands of years. Each has served a useful purpose in the achievement of Chinese culture, and each is essential to the other two. *Jen*, as the prime virtue of life, leads the way to prompting men to positive efforts for the good of others. *Yi* follows, to collaborate with *jen*, as the high-

---
[1] *Analects*, II, 3.

est principle embodied in the activities of mankind. And *li*, as the outward expression of moral sentiment, sheds light on *jen* and *yi*, bringing the whole conduct into harmony with reason and order, thus completing the temple of Confucianism.

Finally, it is necessary to bear in mind that the philosophies of Confucius and Mencius and Hsün Tzŭ are all predominantly ethical, devoted to social relations and civil duties. Although in Hsün Tzŭ's book there is a chapter "On Heaven," its purpose is not to praise supernatural mysteries but to deny the existence of spiritual beings whom the ceremonies were supposed to honor. With Hsün Tzŭ, Heaven was depersonalized and conceived as naturalistic law—what Lao Tzŭ would call *Tao*. This conception cast man upon his own resources and challenged him to make himself master of nature.

> If the right way of life is cultivated, then Heaven cannot send misfortune; flood and drought cannot cause famine; extreme cold or heat cannot cause suffering; supernatural powers cannot cause calamity.

On the other hand, if man should neglect his duty, Heaven would be helpless to help him. In rejecting supernatural beliefs, Hsün Tzŭ in fact succeeded in completing the development of Confucianism into a naturalistic humanism. This monumental act of completion is the most accurate indication of Hsün Tzŭ's achievement.

Han Fei Tzŭ

"A state cannot be strong forever, nor can it remain weak. When its laws are strictly administered, the state is strong. When its laws are loosely administered, it is weak."
Han Fei Tzŭ, Ch. 19.

8. Han Fei Tzŭ

We have seen that in the Chou period various schools of thought developed, all concerned with the achievement of an ideal human society. There was Confucianism, with its leading exponents and formulators: Confucius, Mencius, and Hsün Tzŭ. They insisted on the maintenance of proper ceremonies and the display by the ruling class of good moral example. On the other hand, there was Taoism, as set forth by Lao Tzŭ and Chuang Tzŭ. They advocated an ideal society to be achieved by abandoning the elaborate ceremonies and organization of current civilization for a return to primitivity so as to conform with the simplicity of the invariable *Tao*. In addition to these two main views, there were other patterns of thought, as represented by the teachings of Yang Chu and Mo Tzŭ. The former deprecated social institutions. He maintained that the only things that make life worth living are sensual gratifications such as the pleasures of food and dress and the enjoyment of music and beauty. Mo Tzŭ, on the other hand, expressed absolute faith in social institutions and enunciated a theory for the organization of society upon the great principle of all-embracing love. One school remains to be considered. It completes our picture of the most significant period in the history of Chinese thought.

Just as the southern temperament was akin to the romantic naturalism of Lao Tzŭ and Chuang Tzŭ, and the people on the central plains were attracted to the humanistic doctrine of the mean as advocated by Confucius and his followers, so the hard-headed northerners clung to Legalist theories and practices.

Flourishing in the third century before the Christian era, when the wars between feudal states increased in intensity, the Legalists despaired of saving the world by elaborate ceremonies, abstract principles or supernatural sanctions. They held that the disjointed and unruly feudal system must give place to a social order held together by drastic regulations strictly administered. Hence, they developed the idea of positive law, distinct from religious and moral sanctions. Fundamental to Legalism was the exaltation of the state at the expense of individuals. Among the Legalists, Han Fei Tzŭ was by far the most celebrated. By no means more original than other members of the school, he did combine the qualities of a laborious scholar and acute thinker, and he knew how to gather the harvest of his predecessors. It is for this reason that he has been chosen to represent the Legalist school. From the outset, it should be noted that, although Han Fei Tzŭ was a great exponent of Legalist thought, his mental activity was stimulated and inspired by the teachings of the great schools of Confucianism, Taoism and

Mohism. His significance arises from the fact that all the Legalist elements and ideas of the fourth and third centuries B.C. reappear transfigured in his system.

[1]

LIFE AND WRITINGS

Han Fei Tzŭ came of a royal family in the state of Han. The date of his birth is a matter of doubt, but his death has been placed at about 233 B.C., when he was approximately fifty years old. This would make his birth year between 282 and 280 B.C. A brilliant teacher and a writer, he was, together with Li Ssŭ, chief minister in the reign of the first Emperor of the Ch'in dynasty (256–221 B.C.), a pupil of Hsün Tzŭ. We find when we come to study Legalist thought that Hsün Tzŭ's theory of human nature must have provided a good psychological basis for the Legalist argument that law should replace morality in restraining the "state of violence." Han Fei Tzŭ's youth coincided with the most disastrous period in the history of his native state of Han. Han, as we have seen, was one of the three fragments into which the state of Tsin broke toward the close of the fifth century B.C. Being the smallest of the principal combatants, her army suffered many reverses and disasters, and her territory was at the mercy of her powerful neighbors. What was worse, here as elsewhere, the state was tyrannized by powerful clans, struggling against one another for supremacy. These facts had an important bearing upon the history of the Legalist theorist's life.

An aristocrat, both in thought and by birth, Han Fei Tzŭ stood for firm and aristocratic government and for laws as the framework of the social order. He recognized the danger to which Han was exposed and comprehended the urgency of immediate action. He then went to see the prince and told him that Han could not afford any longer to be a weak, unorganized state in the face of enemy attacks. But the prince did not listen to his advice, nor did he take him into his service. Disappointed and disgusted, Han Fei Tzŭ seems to have retired into private life and persevered in research and in writing. In the *Historical Records* of Ssŭ-ma Ch'ien, we read:

> Therefore Han Fei was quite disgusted at the prince who did not govern the state by force expressed in law, and who did not exercise absolute authority over ministers and subordinates. The way of enriching and strengthening the state consists in employing those who are good and capable, but the prince vested honors and power on those who were dissipated and worthless. . . . He complained that when the country was at peace, the prince supported scholars. But when difficulties arose, he had to use warriors. Thus, those who were supported were not those who were used, and those who were used were not those who had been supported. Mourning over the loyal and the good to whom the wicked ministers were opposed and on the basis of the experience of the past, Han Fei Tzŭ wrote down his teachings.

In his writings, Confucian scholars are portrayed as academic theorists, out of touch with the realities of the time and failing to comprehend the perversity and wrongdoing of the people. Han Fei Tzŭ was emphatic in believing that government must be based upon "the actual facts of the world as it now exists," having no desire to experiment with these scholars' impractical theories of government.

> At the present time, scholars discussing the imperial rule do not speak of the conditions of this government but of the merits of past governments. They do not investigate the facts of official laws nor do they examine the perverted conditions of the people but talk about traditions of ancient times. Holding up for emulation the merits of earlier rulers, the scholars say in elegant language, "Listen to our advice and you will be a valiant monarch." Such words are like the prayers of sorcery. Rulers of capacity will not accept such advice. The intelligent sovereign looks at realities and discards what is useless. He does not discourse upon human-heartedness and righteousness, nor does he listen to the advice of scholars.*

But it was the first emperor of the Ch'in dynasty who first attempted to reorganize China according to Han Fei Tzŭ's teachings. In the *Historical Records* of Ssŭ-ma Ch'ien, it is recorded that when two of the philosopher's essays, entitled "Solitary Indignation" and

---

* All extracts in this chapter are from the *Han Fei Tzŭ*, unless otherwise noted.

"The Five Vermin," came accidentally into the hands of the Emperor, he exclaimed to his ministers:

> This is just what I have been looking for. If the author can become attached to my court, I shall have no regrets in my life.

As we have already seen, the Ch'in state had adopted the policy of seeking the best talents of neighboring states for viziers and generals, so that in the middle of the third century B.C. professional scholars flocked into the court. Thus it was that Li Ssŭ, a native of the Ch'u state, became a minister of Ch'in. Han Fei Tzŭ, however, was a patriot and remained loyal to his native state. Although the prince of Han had not taken the scholar-statesman into his service. Han Fei Tzŭ still would not give his great abilities to the service of a rival state.

In the first half of the third century B.C. Ch'in repeatedly defeated its formidable rival, the state of Ch'u, and annexed much of its territory. The final victory was with the assistance of Li Ssŭ, Han Fei Tzŭ's fellow student and now a minister in the court of Ch'in. Han, which was Ch'in's nearest neighbor, would be the first to be swallowed in order to assure Ch'in the empire. The energy of Li Ssŭ was directed toward achieving this when Han Fei Tzŭ was sent to Ch'in as a good-will envoy from Han. He was so well received in that court that the officials, including Li Ssŭ, became jealous. They slandered him to the king with the result that the honored visitor was accused of treachery and thrown into prison.

Then Li Ssŭ sent him some poison and advised him to commit suicide. Han Fei Tzŭ wanted to confess before the king but had no chance to procure an interview. When the king repented of his action and gave orders to set him free, Han Fei Tzŭ had already died in prison.[1]

The life of Han Fei Tzŭ covered the transition period from the Chou dynasty to the Ch'in dynasty. It was a decisive transition that was leading to a change in the social structure of China. About 250 B.C., Ch'in was not only one of the strongest economically among the feudal states but had already made an end of its own feudal system. Ch'in was ruled on the principles of the Legalist school, which were best adapted to the new economic and social situation. It was but natural, then, that the teachings of Han Fei Tzŭ were to serve as a philosophical basis for the future greatness of the Ch'in state.

His teachings have been preserved in a book bearing his name and consisting of fifty-five essays of considerable value. These essays contain a complete synthesis of the Legalist ideas of the fourth and third centuries B.C.

However, before considering Han Fei Tzŭ further, it would be best to look at the school of Legalism as a whole.

---

[1] Ssŭ-ma Ch'ien, *Historical Records*.

[2]

EXPONENTS AND BRANCHES OF LEGALISM

Legalism did not originate with Han Fei Tzŭ. There are scholars who insist that the first formulator of Legalism was Kuan Ch'ung, a well-known minister in the state of Ch'i in the seventh century B.C. Kuan Ch'ung not only made Ch'i the richest and strongest state in the east by levying taxes upon salt and iron, but also established a pattern of good and efficient administration. However, it is doubtful if any part of the philosophical work under the name of *Kuan Tzŭ* is attributable to Kuan Ch'ung. Its date and authorship are alike unknown, but it is generally believed that the work was produced by scholars of the Legalist school in the latter part of the Warring States period—about 250 B.C. According to the note in the *Catalog* of Liu Hsin (about 1 A.D.), the work consisted of eighty-six essays of which ten are now lost. Kuan Ch'ung was in fact a practical statesman and he stressed propriety, justice, prudence and temperance, which typified the rational thought of the Spring and Autumn period. He favored vigorous administration that accorded with the ideals of the Legalists. Thus, the position of Kuan Ch'ung in Legalism is somewhat analogous to that of Chou Kung or the Duke of Chou in Confucianism. It was for this reason that Han Fei Tzŭ referred to Kuan Ch'ung with reverence.

Another important figure was Tzŭ-ch'an, prime minister of Chêng, who promulgated the first written Chinese code as early as 536 B.C. When he was in power, all the people gladly accepted his reforms and none transgressed his prohibitions. Order prevailed in the state, and the neighboring princes treated Chêng with proper respect.

In the actual formation of the Legalist school, three men took the lead: Shên Tao of Chao, Shên Pu-hai of Han and Shang Yang of Wei. They all were prominent Legalist thinkers, living in the fourth century B.C. in the northern secessionist states.

To begin with, Shên Tao, also known as Shên Tzŭ, was a native of the Chao state. The dates of his birth and death are unknown, but it is believed that he was a contemporary of Mencius. He is known in the Legalist school as the advocate of the doctrine that *shih* or "authority" is the most important factor in politics and government. In the *Han Fei Tzŭ* there is a passage, quoted from the writings of Shên Tao, that offers a good illustration of the concept of *shih:*

. . . the good yield to the wicked because of slight authority and low position. The wicked keep the good in subjection because of supreme authority and high position. When Yao [the sage-king] was a commoner, he could not rule three men. On the other hand, when Chieh [the wicked ruler] was Emperor, he could throw the world into confusion. Hence, I know that *shih* [authority] and position are indispensable and that good and wisdom are not dependable. We cannot shoot high with a weak bow even though we have the force of the wind with us. The wicked can enforce his orders with the support of the multitude. When Yao was a subordinate, the people would not listen to his instructions. When he became the Emperor, his orders were obeyed and his injunctions executed. From these premises, it seems clear that good and wisdom cannot keep the populace in subjection, but *shih* and position can.

The point is that *shih* is what enables a ruler to govern; and it is exactly this that we find in the work of Kuan Tzŭ:

When the wise sovereign governs with absolute authority, the ministers abstain from all wrongs. Then, they dare not betray the sovereign, not because they love him, but because they are afraid of his authority. The people are ready to offer their services, not because of their love for the sovereign, but because they are afraid of his authority. Thus, the wise sovereign, who stands in a high position, can rule the people; and he who holds absolute authority can restrain the ministers. Then, orders are obeyed; and injunctions, executed. The sovereign is held in esteem and the ministers are kept in subjection. Therefore, the law says: "Esteem the sovereign and humble the ministers, not because there is special affection, but because there is supreme authority."

The theory of emphasizing princely power served as the basis for absolute monarchy and represents one of the branches of the Legalist school.

Another branch is embodied in the figure of Shên Pu-hai, also called Shên Tzŭ, who was a minister of the state of Han. His working life fell mostly in the second half of the fourth century B.C. He advanced the concept of *shu* as an indispensable element in government. *Shu* is the art of government or statecraft by means of which a ruler controls his subordinates and employs them to his own advantage. In dealing with *shu* and the administration of the state, Shên Pu-hai seemed to follow the path of the Taoists. In the *Lu Shih Ch'un Ch'iu*, or the *Spring and Autumn of Lu Pu-wei* (*c*. 235 B.C.) we read:

> Shên Pu-hai said: ". . . give no ear and you can hear without listening; close the eye and you can discern without seeing; and forego intelligence and you can be just without knowledge. The abandonment of these three is the way of government; their retention is the way of anarchy. The ear, eye and intelligence are not dependable. What can be learned from them is deficient and inadequate. What is deficient and inadequate cannot restrain and guide the people. . . . Therefore, the most intelligent man will discard intelligence; the most benevolent man will forget benevolence; and the virtuous man will think not of virtue. Keep silent and think nothing; just wait and bide the time and success will be achieved. . . . Thus, the ruler who needs

not suggest will be agreed with. He who needs not commence will be followed. Therefore, the ancient kings did little and nevertheless caused much to be done. What causes much to be done is the *shu* of the sovereign; what is to be done is the *Tao* of the ministers. From this premise, I come to the conclusions: 'Ignorance and inaction are much better than knowledge and action. This is the way of the sovereign.' "

This teaching appears at first to illustrate fairly orthodox Taoist doctrine—that of *wu wei* (inaction or noninterference). However, as recognized by Han Fei Tzŭ, it was really a means of keeping subordinates in submission. *Shu*, when applied in practical terms, consisted of certain covert methods on the part of the ruler effected upon a submissive do-nothing public.

One other member of the Legalist school should be mentioned. Shang Yang, popularly known as the Lord of Shang, was a man of affairs and yet a profound student and painstaking researcher in the history of political institutions. Although he belonged to the ruling family of Wei, he spent most of his active life in the public service of Ch'in, in the middle of the fourth century B.C. It was largely through his influence that Ch'in attained sufficient power to prepare the way for its ultimate triumph. He is said to have reformed everything, from army discipline to land tenure, and to have reorganized the laws and administration. The philosophical work under his name is possibly of a later period, but it is believed that at least part of it is attributable to him.

He is reported to have advocated what were then called "the arts of agriculture and war." According to Shang Yang, food production and military preparation were the activities that the state should support; the farmers and soldiers, the only classes of citizens that the state should encourage. Since agriculture is toilsome and war dangerous, he advised his prince to "bring about a condition where people would find it bitter not to till the soil and where they would find it dangerous not to fight." He detested the Confucian scholars because he felt they were good for nothing but the study of poetry and history.

> If in a country there are the following ten things: odes and history, rites and music, virtue and cultivation thereof, filial piety and fraternity and prudence, then the ruler will have nobody to employ for defense and warfare. If a country is governed by means of these ten things, it will be dismembered as soon as an enemy approaches. And even if no enemy approaches, the country will be poor.[2]

His greatest achievement, however, was the strict administration of *fa* (law), another important Legalist concept. He is reported to have enacted a set of new laws with exact rewards and punishments in which he neither spared the strong and great in their pun-

---
[2] *Shang Chun*, Ch. 1.

ishments nor showed favoritism to relatives and friends. Clearly, Shang Yang's ideas were much the best suited to the conditions of the breakdown of feudalism during the Warring States period. So it was that the Legalists, rather than the Confucians, gained the upper hand in the politics of the turbulent period.

Han Fei Tzŭ's stature must be measured in the light of the teachings of Shên Tao, Shên Pu-hai and Shang Yang. He appropriated the ideas of *shih*, *shu* and *fa* and developed them, always guided by a brilliant and original principle of his own.

> A state cannot be strong forever, nor can it remain weak. When its laws are strictly administered, the state is strong. When its laws are loosely administered, the state is weak.

Han Fei Tzŭ always maintained this—that a well-governed state primarily depends on a fixed body of laws, strictly and firmly administered. This body or code of laws must be lengthy and detailed:

> If their textbook is too summary, pupils will twist its meaning; if a law is too concise, the people will dispute its intentions. Hence, the sage when he writes a book sets forth its arguments fully and clearly. An enlightened ruler when he makes his laws sees to it that every contingency is provided for in detail.

Not only this but the penalties provided in the code must be very heavy.

> Shang Yang instituted heavy punishments for minor wrongs. Capital crimes are seldom committed, but minor wrongs are frequent. The best policy for government is to lead the people to avoid what is easy and so not to commit what is difficult. When there are no minor wrongs, there will be no capital crimes. . . . Therefore, Kung-sun Yang [Shang Yang] said: "If the punishments are heavy, no one will dare transgress the law; this is the way of eliminating crimes by penalty."

The law cannot of course work merely mechanically. It requires men to operate it. These men should employ *shu* or statecraft:

> Shên Pu-hai emphasized *shu* and Kung-sun Yang stressed *fa*. By *shu* we mean that positions are filled by appointment, rank being ascertained according to merit. Hence, there are means of inflicting penalties and there is power for restraining the ministers. This is what the sovereign should possess. By *fa* we mean that all regulations and punishments are enacted. Hence, those who obey the law will be rewarded; those who violate the law will be punished. This is what the ministers should conform to. When the sovereign does not have *shu*, there is danger in the government. When the ministers do not conform to *fa*, there

is violence among the people. Neither can be dispensed with, for both are the implements of the sovereign.

In addition to *fa* and *shu* there must also be *shih*, in the sense of princely power or authority. According to Han Fei Tzŭ, *shih* is what enables a sovereign to "enforce his strict orders." A king without *shih* is therefore not much different from any ordinary man; he is powerless to enforce his orders and make his influence felt among the people. *Shih* comes to the king automatically from "the mere fact of his being king"; he needs no moral qualities or special capacities. In an interesting allegory, Han Fei Tzŭ compared the *shih* of a monarch to the sharp teeth and claws of tigers and leopards; without *shih* a king would be helpless and crippled as these beasts would be without teeth and claws.

In short, by integrating the works of various philosophers, Han Fei Tzŭ sought to build up his Legalist theory which, although not preserved entirely, left a permanent impression on Chinese political thinking and institutions.

[3]

GENERAL ASPECTS OF "HANFEISM"

Han Fei Tzŭ was a man of the widest learning. Although classified with the Legalists, he was in many respects a Taoist—principally because he advocated the doctrine of *wu wei*.

> Just as the sun and moon shine forth, the four seasons progress, the clouds spread and the wind blows, so does the ruler not encumber his mind with knowledge or himself with selfishness. He relies for good government on *fa* and *shu*, leaves right and wrong to be dealt with through rewards and punishments, and refers lightness and heaviness to the balance of the scale.

In other words, once the ruler possesses the implements and mechanism through which government is conducted, everything will happen of its own accord.

Moreover, Han Fei Tzŭ studied under Hsün Tzŭ, the great Confucian scholar, and so was subject to some Confucian ideas. In the early Chinese feudal society, the nobles had been governed according to *li* (rites), but the common people had been governed solely by *hsing* (punishment). Confucius, however, had insisted on discarding the latter and on applying *li* to everyone. True to this and the Legalist conception, Han Fei Tzŭ also held that there should be equal application of the law to nobles and serfs.

> Ministers are never exempt from punishment for their faults; commoners are never overlooked in rewards for good.

Instead of elevating the common people to a higher standing, however, Han Fei Tzŭ lowered the nobles by discarding *li* and applying *hsing* to all alike. And again, we find that the teachings of Han Fei

Tzŭ had some things in common with those of Mo Tzŭ. Han Fei Tzŭ said:

> A state under an enlightened sovereign does not provide for trivial documents but promulgates a code of laws for the guidance of the people; nor does it follow the ways of early kings but makes the governing officials the people's masters; nor does it tolerate private feuds but gets the people to die in fighting wars. In such a state, everyone abides by the law, works hard for the state, and delights in fighting.

This is similar to Mo Tzŭ's theory on the need for uniformity.

In spite of this extensive use of others' materials, it is important to recognize Han Fei Tzŭ not as an eclectic but as an individualist who was highly original in his thought.

To begin with, he rejected the static conception of history. His position stemmed from his observation of the changes and progress of the world. Most strikingly, the old order had passed away and a new China was emerging. In a like manner, his thought became an effort to disregard traditional authority and to adjust social and political institutions to the changing circumstances. In his most famous chapter, that entitled "The Five Vermin," Han Fei Tzŭ remarked on the changing, evolutionary nature of history. He recalled that once men had built houses in trees to protect themselves from the beasts and wildlife and that they had been overjoyed with the success of this plan. Similarly, once men had marveled at the fact that fire could be produced by rubbing two pieces of wood together. But, Han Fei Tzŭ argued, people who would now live in trees or produce fire in the old method would be jeered at, for new and better things had been discovered. He concluded:

> And so today if there were someone who lauded the ways of Yao, Shun, Yü, T'ang and Wu [the five sage sovereigns of old] to the present generation, he would be laughed at by the modern sages. Hence, the sage does not aim at practicing antiquity, nor at setting up principles. Rather, he studies the affairs of his own age and then devises means of meeting them accordingly.

We have seen how Confucius appealed to Yao and Shun for authority, how the Taoists claimed descent from Huang Ti (the Yellow Emperor) and how the Mohists revered the great Yü as their master. In their stress on the past, these philosophers created a static conception of history. The veneration of antiquity, although it contributed to continuity and stability, interfered with new ideas and the forces of progress. It resulted in an overbalanced conservatism, which Han Fei Tzŭ had been quick to recognize and most emphatically condemn. For he considered history as a process of change.

Laws should move with the progress of the time,

and government should conform to the exigencies of the present.

By way of illustration of the folly of appealing to the past, Han Fei Tzŭ told a story:

> There was once a man of Sung who tilled his field. In the middle of the field was a tree stump. One day a rabbit, in full course, ran head on into the stump, broke its neck and died. Thereupon, the man left his plow and stood waiting at that tree in the hope that he would catch more rabbits. But, naturally, he never caught another and was laughed at by the people of Sung. If, however, you wish to rule the people of today by the methods of government of the early kings, you do exactly the same thing. . . . Therefore, affairs go according to their time, and preparations are made in accordance with affairs.

Han Fei Tzŭ's cynical theory of human nature, as mentioned above, provided good psychological basis for Legalist ideas. In fact, the theory was a nearly inevitable outgrowth of the chaos of the time. Han Fei Tzŭ's response was similar. He had studied the history of political institutions and was familiar with the inner politics of the turbulent states. He concluded that man is essentially selfish and materialistic. He even went on to state that the relationship between parents and children is permeated by a desire for advantage.

There is something more than love in the relationship of parents with their children. If a son is born, they congratulate each other. If a daughter is born, they [may] kill it. Both have come out of the mother's womb; yet, when it is a boy, congratulations ensue; when it is a girl, death! The parents are thinking of convenience later on, and they calculate on long-term profit. So it is that even parents in their relationship with their children have calculating minds and treat the children accordingly.

Then Han Fei Tzŭ warned his prince not to place confidence in those about him:

The sovereign is exposed to danger by placing confidence in his ministers; he who confides in men will certainly be dominated by men. Ministers, in their relations to the sovereign, have no tie of kinship but serve him solely because constrained by the force of circumstances. Therefore, ministers always watch the mental condition of their master; whereas the lord remains idle and arrogant over them. . . . Also, if the lord has much confidence in his son, wicked ministers will utilize the son to accomplish their own selfish purposes. . . . If the lord has much confidence in his wife, the wicked ministers will utilize her to accomplish their own ends. . . . If he cannot trust in the love of his wife and the affection of his son, who else can be more dependable?

He supported his argument with a variety of examples:

> The servant works for the master not because he is faithful but because he is paid for his work. Similarly, the master treats the servant well not because he is kind but because he engages the servant's service. Hence, their hearts are centered on utility, and they both harbor the idea of serving themselves.

Han Fei Tzŭ concluded:

> One gives and receives for his own selfish purpose. If there is common interest, men, even though they are strangers, will live in harmony. Conversely, if their interests conflict with one another, even if they be father and son, they will strive against one another.

Thus, conformity with man's natural disposition leads to all kinds of violence and disorder. Only under the restraint of severe laws and heavy punishments does man live in peace and harmony. In advising the sovereign how best to maintain his authority, Han Fei Tzŭ warned him not to discourse upon human-heartedness and righteousness, but "to guide the people by laws and enforce the laws by punishments"—the two handles of government over which the lord should have firm control.

Although the teachings of Mencius and the Legalists

differ widely, they both emphasized the material standard of living of the people. True to the Legalist conception, Han Fei Tzǔ maintained that an economically solid population was the basis of a good state.

> In the past when men did not plow, they had plenty of natural kernels and grains to eat. When women did not weave, they had plenty of furs and feathers to wear. Though not engaged in labor, they lived on rich food. All that was because men were few and things many. Therefore, there was no quarrel among the people. So it was that even without large rewards and heavy punishments, the people could be kept in peace. Now, suppose there is a man who has five sons, each of whom in turn has five. Then, even during the life of the grandfather, there are already twenty-five descendants. Suddenly, therefore, men are many and things few. The people, though they work hard, live on poor food. This leads to quarrels among the people. . . . Thus, the moderns strive against one another not because they are wicked but that things are few.

While this can serve as still further justification for strong government, it is an interesting indication of the emphasis Han Fei Tzǔ placed on material prosperity. Of course, this idea was not new. Confucius taught that the state must "enrich the people." Mencius was concerned with improving the people's lot by means of reforms such as land tenure and reduction of taxes.

Hsün Tzŭ spoke of the balance between men's material wants and the supply of these necessities. Mo Tzŭ advocated an economy of expenditure. But the Legalists, as typified by Han Fei Tzŭ, stressed agriculture and economic self-sufficiency for the purpose of welding the state into an effective unit.

> One who cultivates the land enjoys wealth; one who fights against enemies wins power.

He maintained that a prince should, on the one hand, "force agricultural labor and the breaking of new land in order to increase the people's wealth; and," on the other hand, "teach military skill to all within the domain, reviewing drills, so that the people might give assistance in times of sudden attack."

[4]

VIEWS ON AN IDEAL HUMAN SOCIETY

Overpopulation and the selfishness of the people, as already mentioned, are two of the greatest causes of confusion and misery in society. In addition, Han Fei Tzŭ accused the "academic theorists," whom the sovereign supported with taxes collected from the hard-working people and who, thoroughly absorbed in their studies but knowing little else, were too proud to demean themselves by undertaking manual labor. He applied this to the people as well:

> Today everyone in the domain talks about govern-

ment and there is not a family that does not possess a copy of the laws of Kuan Tzŭ and Shang Tzŭ. But despite this, the land grows poorer and poorer. This is because those who talk about agriculture are many; those who hold the plow are few. Everyone in the domain talks about the art of warfare . . . but our armies grow weaker and weaker. This is because those who talk about fighting are many; those who put on armor are few.

In addition, the existing intellectual anarchy, Han Fei Tzŭ claimed, "not only stirs up confusion about the actual conditions of society but also awakens distrust in the state."

The sovereign listens to the spurious learnings and dissident discussions. Hence, there is no standard for discourse, nor is there any rule for action. Ice and coal cannot be put in the same place, nor can winter and summer come at the same time. By the same reasoning, opposing schools of learning cannot prevail and flourish without dissension. But the sovereign listens to these dissident learnings and he practices opposing doctrines. How can there be no violence?

Han Fei Tzŭ's way to an ideal society consisted first, in forcing "agricultural labor and the breaking of new land in order to increase the people's wealth"; second, in "developing punishments and employing penalties in order to control the depraved"; third, in "imposing taxes and levying excises, filling the granaries and treasuries so as to eliminate famine and support the army" and fourth, in "teaching military skill to all within the domain, reviewing the drills, to defend the country against aggressors."

With this general picture in mind, Han Fei Tzŭ divided the social order into two groups: the useful people and the idle. Among the former were the farmers and warriors, the only classes that society should honor and encourage. Among the latter were the corrupted nobles and unrealistic scholars, whom Han Fei Tzŭ condemned as parasites. He particularly detested the Confucians because they diverted those who might have been farmers and fighters into the ranks of scholars, good for nothing but "adorning themselves with polite literature and learned discourse." Hence, the rulers, he insisted, should suppress the scholars' doctrinaire theories for the good of the people, who should be engaged in the productive pursuit of agriculture and the "honorable" profession of soldiery.

> The rulers in taking [the theories] from the learned, if they hold the theories to be true, ought to promulgate them and appoint the learned to office. If they hold the theories to be false, they ought to discard them and to terminate their principles. Nowadays, however, the rulers do not give official recognition to what they hold to be true. Nor do they discard and terminate what they hold to be false. This acceptance without

application and doubt without reaction surely constitute the road to perdition.

In short, the social policies of Han Fei Tzŭ were aimed at the exaltation of the farmer-warrior class and the condemnation of the official-scholar class. It should be observed that while these policies had little or nothing to do with the old idea of the feudal state, they were well suited to the new times. The population of Ch'in, organized throughout according to these policies, gained supremacy in agriculture and war. As a result, Ch'in succeeded in removing one opponent after another until they had brought about a unification of China for the first time in her history.

[5]

AN ESTIMATE

Han Fei Tzŭ instituted an elaborate program that contemplated a thoroughgoing reorganization of the social and political policy of the state. The program was accompanied by important innovations in "the arts of agriculture and war." Its purpose was primarily to increase the wealth of the people and the military power of the state in its struggle for hegemony. The main features of Han Fei Tzŭ's political program may be summarized as follows:

1. An absolute monarchy under the sovereign through a bureaucracy.
2. Economic self-sufficiency of each principality.

3. Administration of severe laws with exact rewards and punishments.

His ideal state, therefore, was a centralized one with one sovereign, one regime, one supreme law—an autocracy that would put an end to all the violence and confusion caused by the breakup of feudalism. These principles were first adopted by the state of Ch'in, where the old idea of the feudal state had been least developed. They succeeded to the extent that while the Ch'in dynasty itself was short-lived its political institutions based on the Legalist theory lasted over a period of 2000 years.

The writings of Han Fei Tzŭ, because they indicated the new questions at issue and the new mental attitude, heralded modern political thinking. Men were viewed as essentially selfish, and the state was exalted at the expense of the individual. Han Fei Tzŭ also developed the idea of positive law as distinct from religious and moral sanction. In the impartial administration of laws, in the institution of centralized bureaucracy and in the emphasis on the economic basis of society, he not only made a great contribution to political philosophy but also impressed on the thought of the Chinese a more scientific view of government. However, although the new Legalist-oriented regime obtained consolidation and stability under a government in the form of paternal despotism, it failed to provide any foundation for the institution of democracy for which modern China has been striving.

The Legalist theory served to uphold the absolutism

of the sovereign at a time when obedience and discipline, rather than freedom, were needed. It taught the people not to discuss or think but to obey, when they were not yet ready to govern themselves. Clearly, these theories were much better suited to the conditions of the breakup of feudalism, even though they were not in accord with democratic principles.

But Han Fei Tzŭ's opinion on this point was simple and clear:

> The sage does not expect to follow ancient ways, nor to set up invariable principles. Rather, he studies the affairs of his own age and devises means of meeting them accordingly.

While Han Fei Tzŭ's policies were then successfully adopted, this important qualification was forgotten.

Conclusion:
Chinese Philosophy over the Ages

After the Chou dynasty, Chinese philosophy falls naturally into four periods. The first is the Ch'in-Han period (about the third century B.C.), when Chinese philosophy, particularly Confucianism, suffered a decline in vitality and appeal. In a sense, this period, with its stress on unity both in the intellectual and political spheres, was an inevitable reaction to the wide freedom of the late Chou years, as characterized by the "hundred schools." And it was in the spirit of this reaction that the Ch'in emperor, Shih Huang Ti, sought to control thought by the abovementioned notorious decree for burning all writings of the "hundred schools," with the exception of works on medicine, divination and agriculture.

While agreeing with the Ch'in dynasty's basic goal of homogeneity, the succeeding Han dynasty (206 B.C.–220 A.D.) disapproved of harsh measures such as those exercised by Shih Huang Ti. In the year 136 B.C., Tung Chung-shu (*c.* 179–104 B.C.) the greatest of the early Han scholars, proposed to the emperor that unity be sought by new means—by the elevation of Confucianism at the expense of the other schools of thought.

But the Confucianism expounded by Tung Chung-shu and adopted in the early Han period was something quite different from that originally set forth by the Sage and his immediate followers. Han Confucianism was tinged by ideas of the rival schools, especially of Taoism. Mohism had not survived the Ch'in suppression, and Legalism had fallen into disgrace, even though elements of its political theory lingered wistfully on in the thinking of the ruling class. Taoism, however, had become influential in government circles to the extent that the *wu wei* doctrine, which is essentially a laissez-faire theory, was adopted as state policy and that Taoist occultism became an often-held personal creed. This fact determined the general character of Han Confucianism.

Generally speaking, the Han scholars divided themselves into two groups. The first was known as the "New Script School" because its version of the classics was written in the form of the then current script. The other was called the "Old Script School" because it claimed to possess the ancient texts that existed before the time of the Ch'in fire. The controversy between these schools turned out to be one of the greatest in the history of Chinese scholarship. Their textual disagreement was accentuated by a difference in their views about the true significance of Confucius and Confucianism. The New Script School considered Confucius as a "throneless king" and a savior of the world, as described in apocryphal literature. In opposition to this view, the Old Script School maintained that Confucius was simply a sage who had given new interpretations to the cultural legacy of the past before transmitting it to posterity. Although the views of the New Script School now seem absurd and vain, they became popular in the Han period mainly because the circumstances of the times were favorable to forgery. Monetary rewards, imperial favor and popular esteem, all encouraged zealous scholars to exercise their inventive faculties to produce plausible substitutes for lost books in the form of New Script texts. Zeal for a revival of the Confucian school may be counted as another motive that led scholars not to scruple over expressing their own ideas in the name of Confucius. This absurdity of the New Script School, more than anything else, was responsible for its ultimate decline in the second half of the Han dynasty. Meanwhile, the influences of Taoism had spread, together with that of Buddhism, which had been introduced from India in the first century A.D., or even earlier; and Chinese philosophy blossomed anew during the ensuing period.

From the third to the tenth centuries, Chinese civilization began to be infused with the cultures of foreign countries. The philosophical thought can be represented by the Taoist metaphysics of the Wei-Chin period (220–420 A.D.) (known as the *hsüan hsüeh* in Chinese or literally, "mysterious learning") and Buddhism of the Sui (581–618 A.D.) and T'ang (618–907 A.D.) dynasties, which had little connection with politics but exercised a great influence on Chinese culture. During the period, Chinese Taoism and Buddhism of Indian origin overshadowed Confucianism. Indeed, Buddhist scriptures, translated into Chinese, grew to vast proportions, and temples and monks multiplied so rapidly that they had to be checked by imperial decree in 845, when 40,000 Buddhist temples were demolished, 260,000 monks and nuns were secularized, and a tremendous acreage of land belonging to the temples was confiscated.

Here it should be noted that there is a distinction between the terms "Chinese Buddhism" and "Buddhism in China." Briefly, "Buddhism in China," as represented by the School of Subjective Idealism (known as *hsiang tsung* or *wei-shih tsung* in Chinese, or the Vijnanavada School), is the form of Buddhism that clung to the Indian tradition and played little part in the development of Chinese philosophy. "Chinese Buddhism," as represented by the Middle Path School (known as the *san-lun tsung* in Chinese or the Madhyamika School), is the form of Buddhism that has been close to Chinese thought and has developed in conjunction with Chinese philosophy. The considerable similarity between the Middle Path School of Buddhism and Chinese Taoism led to their interaction with each other and resulted in the *Ch'an* (known as *zen* in Japanese) or the Dhyana School. This similarity is easily seen.

The Chinese term *ch'an* or *ch'an-na* is derived from the Sanskrit *dhyana*, which is usually translated into English as "meditation." Originally, *Ch'an* meant "directly pointing to the human mind and to become a Buddha by seeing one's own Buddha-nature" or "by identifying the individual with the Universal Mind." This was to be achieved through meditation. Ch'anism is the philosophy of silence through its emphasis on a "special transmission outside of the Sacred Teaching." Its meditation doctrine is not based on classic Buddhist scriptures but on enlightenment through "the realization of individual identification with the Universal Mind." Interpretations of the Universal Mind among Ch'an masters are various, but in general it is conceived as "the Void," that is, something that cannot be designated by words or perceived by the senses. Hence, to penetrate the Universal Mind, Ch'an masters either urged *wu nien* or "absence of thought," or advocated *wang ch'ing* or "ignoring our feelings," or they recommended *jen hsin* or "letting the mind follow its own course."

There is so much in common between such ideas and Taoism that the early Buddhist writers used Taoist terminology to express Buddhist ideas: *yü* or "being," *wu* or "nonbeing," *yü wei* or "action," and *wu wei* or "nonaction." "Sudden Enlightenment," which leads to Buddhahood, was often referred to by the Ch'an masters as the "vision of *Tao*."

It is interesting to note that one of the chief contributions of Buddhism to Chinese thought was the doctrine of the Universal Mind, as expounded in the School of Mahayana (known as the *hsing tsung* in Chinese or School of Universal Mind). This doctrine assumed an important role in the Neo-Confucianism of the Sung-Ming period.

The period of the Sung (960–1280 A.D.) and Ming (1368–1644 A.D.) dynasties was noted for the rise of *Li Hsüeh Chia* or the school of study of *li*, usually known in the West as Neo-Confucianism. However, the term "Neo-Confucianism" is a misnomer since it does not stand here for a genuine revival of Confucianism. The Neo-Confucianists were doubtless Confucian scholars, but their intellectual activity was stimulated and determined by the speculations of Ch'an masters. Thus, Neo-Confucianism was a kind of summing up or revision of the ethics, morals and beliefs of the past, but its principles of Confucianism were thoroughly tinged with Buddhism—just as Buddhism had interacted with Taoism and emerged as Ch'anism, or Confucianism interacted with Buddhism and emerged as Li-ism, or what is called Neo-Confucianism.

The close relationship between Buddhism and Neo-Confucianism may be seen in the following illustrations. The ideal state of *nirvana*, according to pure Buddhists, is a state of mind of stillness. But to the Confucianists, the most essential state is that of permanent activity. Thus, the *Yi Ching* or *Book of Changes* declares:

> The movement of the heavenly bodies is constant, and the superior man seeks to improve himself without rest.

In resolving this difference the Neo-Confucianists formed the conception of "stillness which is in constant activity, and activity which is in constant stillness." There are several illustrations that the Neo-Confucianists liked to cite. The mind is like a mirror; all the varied images that fall upon its surface are unceasingly active while the mirror remains still and is not bewildered. The mind is like the sun; the clouds pass and vanish under it, but the sun remains constant and is not affected. Also, the mind is like the vast surface of the sea; the waves rise and fall over it, but the general level remains calm and is not disturbed. For the mind is not outside the activity; it is in fact the mind that is active; but while it is active it remains still. This union of stillness and activity is the highest and best state of mind.

Moreover, the Buddhists held that the visible world is an illusion, a fiction of the imagination; they regarded it as unreal, empty, the Great Void. But the Confucianists said that there is an objective world, coexisting with man's own subjective idea of it. The Neo-Confucianists resolved this difficulty by accepting that the external world is an "emptiness," a void, while insisting that it had a kind of illusory substantiality. As Chang Tsai (1020–77 A.D.), the great philosopher of the Sung period, said:

> The immensity of space, though called the Great Void, is not void at all. It is filled with *Ch'i* [primordial essence]. In fact there is no such thing as a vacuum.

Ch'i is a concept that became very important in the cosmological and metaphysical theories of the later Neo-Confucianists.

And again, Buddhism is generally regarded as an other-worldly philosophy because it holds that life itself is the root of its own misery, that the present world is but "a sea of bitterness." But Confucianism was very much this-worldly in its outlook and essentially humanistic, occupying itself with human relations and shunning questions of the supernatural. The Neo-Confucianists resolved this conflict by calling both original schools too arbitrary and one-sided. They said that Buddhism was too idealistic and divine while Confucianism was too realistic and humanistic, and they attempted a synthesis between these two extremes.

However, a divergence of thought did emerge and ultimately led to the formation of two separate schools, the rationalistic or Sung School, and the idealistic or Ming School. Generally speaking, the Sung was nearer to the whole rationale of Confucian thought; the Ming, to Indian Buddhism. The Ming School accused the Sung Neo-Confucianists of being too formal; the Sung School accused the Ming Neo-Confucianists of being too subjective. And although they both agreed that the "prime doctrine" or "fundamental truth" in the universe is *li* (they were thus close to the Taoist position except in their use of *li* for *Tao* to express the basic idea), they differed in defining this truth. Trying to combine Confucianism with Buddhist thought, the Sung School began by looking out upon the external world and conceived of *li* as Heaven or nature. But the Ming School, purporting to modify Buddhism with Confucian teachings, began by looking inward upon themselves and conceived of *li* as the mind.

In any event, Neo-Confucianism is one of the most important philosophies China has developed. The intellectual influences that had acted upon China in the past, the culture and thought that had been brought from foreign lands, all permeate this body of thought and are crystallized within it.

And lastly, the period of the Manchu dynasty

(1644–1911 A.D.) and that of the Republic (1911–) constitute an age of social disturbance, political instability and intellectual anarchy. The latter period has been so chaotic that it resulted in the emergence in 1949 of two separate Chinese regimes—the Nationalist in Taiwan, the Communist in the mainland.

The whole tendency of this age has been skeptical and destructive, with all established institutions, even such things as marriage and the family, coming in for criticism. The foremost scholar, Liang Ch'i-ch'ao (1873–1929) compared this period to the age of the Renaissance in Europe. Indeed, the general character of thought during the period has been intimately connected with the striking political and social events of the time. Christianity has acquired a firm foothold in China and with it, Western science and philosophy—notably the pragmatism of John Dewey and the dynamic doctrines of Karl Marx. Both have exerted a tremendous influence on Chinese intellectuals. Meanwhile, translations from the works of eminent Western writers such as Tolstoy, Ibsen, De Maupassant, Shelley, Emerson, Marx and Engels have further helped to create a new mental atmosphere.

Philosophy goes hand in hand with political, social, religious and artistic development; all are but different means by which the culture of a country expresses itself. It is natural, then, that during this last period of total change an independent school of criticism has arisen and launched an attack on the Neo-Confucianism of the Sung and Ming periods. These critics are considered the most skeptical and critical that China has produced. But although their extreme critical outlook can be classified as a school of pragmatism, it is still not a school of philosophy. The emphasis has been all too much upon linguistic study and textual criticism and far too little upon genuine philosophic enquiry. In time, as a matter of fact, penetrating criticism of this pragmatic movement itself may result in a legitimate new school of Chinese philosophical thought.

The so-called "New Culture" Movement was a later manifestation of this critical spirit. Taking the West's positivism and pragmatism as their great inspiration, and science, social progress and democracy as their chief objectives, the leaders of this movement identified Confucianism with the conservativism of the past. Their rallying cry became "Down with Confucius and his company." But the ideals of several millennia could not be put aside so easily, and a controversy arose that continues, tragically, to the present day.

Once, everything changed except China. Now, there is nothing in China that does not change. The most conservative nation in history has become the most radical, bent upon destroying every time-honored tradition, whether in the form of an institution, a classic or a social and moral norm. Nevertheless, the traditional thought patterns, as molded by the teachings of the ancient philosophers, cannot be eradicated promptly or brainwashed by Marxian ideology. The old philosophical and moral standards persist in the minds of the people. The Chinese prefer compromise, harmony and synthesis—all quite incompatible with Marxian ideology. Recognizing this, the Communists have attempted to modify Marxist-Leninist theory to make it more acceptable to the themes of traditional Chinese humanism.

This is not to say that the story of Chinese philosophy is a static one, for as we have seen, it is anything but that. Chinese philosophy has evolved and changed as much as that of any nation, but the Chinese have rarely borrowed extensively from alien cultures without adapting these borrowings to their particular philosophic patterns. In fact, the most significant characteristics of the development of Chinese thought have been its organic naturalness and harmony. Influences not fitting naturally into this evolutionary process have not survived.

Glossary and Selected Bibliography

Glossary

Ai: 1. Love with gradations (Confucian concept); 2. Love for all, equally and without discrimination (*Chien ai*, Mohist concept).

Ch'an (Japanese, *Zen*) or **Ch'an-na** (Sanskrit, *Dhyana*): Meditations; originally the word for instantaneous intuition of truth.

Ch'ang: Normality; the antithesis of what is artificial, arbitrary and abnormal; the Taoist invariable law of nature.

Ch'anism: Philosophy of silence or meditation, based on above principle of attaining to Buddhahood through sudden enlightenment.

Ch'êng: Honesty; sincerity; truthfulness; being one's true self.

Chêng ming: The rectification of names—a Confucian doctrine holding that names should correspond to actualities.

Ch'i: Life breath; vital force; used in connection with the Neo-Confucianist *li* (eternal principle). The *Ch'i* means matter-energy; i.e., whatever is within the realm of matter.

Ch'i wan wu: Equalization of all things—a Taoist ideal.

Chih: Wisdom, one of the Five Constant Virtues (*Wu ch'ang*); **Liang chih:** intuitive knowledge.

Chün tzu: Lord's son; princely man; originally, noble overlord—later, perfect gentleman or superior man.

Chung shû: Chung: faithfulness or loyalty to one's self; **shu:** consideration or sympathy for the feeling of others; i.e., altruism.

Chung yung: Doctrine of the golden mean as illustrated in the *Book of Chung Yung,* commonly attributed to K'ung Chi or K'ung Tzŭ-ssŭ, grandson of Confucius.

Fa: Law or regulation; one of the Legalist concepts.

Fa Chia: School of the Legalists; Legalism.

Fo Chiao: Buddhist religion; Buddhism as a religion.

Fo hsüeh: Buddhist learning; Buddhism as a philosophy.

Hsiao jen: "Small man" or common man, opposite of *Chün tzŭ;* originally a peasant—later, mean, despicable person.

Hsiao ti Hsiao: Filial piety; love of parents; **ti:** fraternal love; brotherly respect.

Hsin: Good faith, one of the Five Constant Virtues (*Wu Ch'ang*).

Hsüan hsüeh: System of profound and mysterious doctrines advocated by Neo-Taoists of the third and fourth centuries A.D.

Jen: Humanity; human-heartedness; true-manhood; a compound of "two" and "man," stressing the relationship between man and his fellow men; love; benevolence; kindness; charity. *Jen* is the essence of Confucius' ethical teachings.

Ju: Literati; scholars who were versed in the six arts (*Liu Yi*): charioting and archery, history and numbers, music and rituals.

Ju Chia: School of Literati, chiefly based on the teachings of Confucius and the Confucian classics.

Ju Chiao: Teachings or religion of Literati.

Ko wu: Study or investigation of things; rectification of affairs.

Li: 1. Ceremonies or rituals; propriety or code of proper conduct; rules of social conduct. Ritual and music (*yüeh*) are two important institutions in Confucianism; 2. Reason; eternal principle; truth; a basic concept of modern Chinese philosophy. *Li* and *ch'i* are the dualistic principles of Neo-Confucianism; 3. Profit; gain; benefit; opposite of righteousness (*yi*).

Li Hsüeh Chia: School of study of *Li* or *Li-ism*, which in the West is called Neo-Confucianism.

Ming: 1. Fate; destiny; decree of Heaven; 2. Name. (See *Chêng ming*).

Ming Chia: School of Names; Sophists, Logicians or Dialecticians who dealt with problem of relation between *ming* (name) and *shih* (actuality).

Ming fêng: Nominal status; social status; *ming* here means "name" while *fêng* means "duty"; hence, a name is a title that gives a man his definite place in society and defines his relationships with others.

Mo Chia: Mohist School, under the leadership of Mo Tzŭ; Mohism.

Pa Kua: Eight Trigrams as represented by an arrangement of certain mystical symbols consisting of triplet combinations of a straight line and a divided line. These were later combined until there were sixty-four hexagrams. Each hexagram was supposed to be a symbolic representation of one or more phenomena of the universe, either human or natural.

P'u: Unhewn block; unadorned simplicity, being the state of original nature—plain, simple and instinctive.

Glossary / 243

Shang t'ung: Agreement with the superior; Mo Tzŭ's political theory.

Shêng jen: A sage; the wise man; the ideal ruler.

Shêng wang: Sage-king, i.e., a ruler with the quality of "wisdom within and kingliness without."

Shih: Authority and power—an important Legalist concept.

Shih fei: Right and wrong; truth and error.

Shu: Statecraft; craft or tact of a ruler for keeping ministers and the people under control.

Ssŭ tuan: The Four Essentials: human-heartedness (*jen*), righteousness (*yi*), propriety (*li*) and wisdom (*chih*).

Ta Tao: The great Course: Great *Tao*.

Ta tung: Great Commonwealth: Great Union; Great Harmony; The Confucian Utopia.

Tai chi: Great Ultimate or Terminus.

Tao: Way; principle; truth; cosmic order. Confucian *Tao* is ethical in sense and deals with the way of life while the *Tao* or the Taoists is essentially metaphysical and can be taken as an all-embracing first principle for the universe.

244 / Glossary

Tao Chia: The Taoist School; the system based on the teachings of Lao Tzŭ.

Tao Chiao: Taoism as a religion.

Tê: Virtue; power, both in the moral and nonmoral sense.

Tien: Sky; Heaven, both in the physical and supernatural sense.

Tien li: Heavenly reason; divine law; the moral principle of Heaven.

Tien ming: Heavenly order or mandate by authority of which a ruler governs.

Tien ti: Heaven and Earth; the universe; the origin of life.

Tzŭ jan: Naturalness or spontaneity as against artificiality; the natural state, the state of *Tao*.

Wang tao: Kingly way that embodies virtuous government; opposite of *pa tao* (the way of a tyrant).

Wu ching: Five Classics: *Shu* (History), *Shih* (Poetry), *Yi* (Change), *Li* (Rites), *Ch'un Ch'iu* (Spring and Autumn Annals).

Wu hsing: Five Elements: Water, Fire, Wood, Metal, Earth.

Wu lun: Five Relationships: between king and subject, between father and son, between husband and wife, between brothers and friends.

Wu wei: Inaction; inactivity; nonassertion; noninterference.

Yi: 1. Righteousness; what one ought to do as opposed to what one would like to do for profit (*li*); 2. Change; in the *Yi Ching* (*Book of Changes*), *yi* is often used interchangeably with *Tao* in the sense of spontaneity.

Yin yang: Passive and active principles of the universe; the female, negative force and the male, positive force, always contrasting but complementary.

Yin-yang Chia: Yin-Yang School, believing in the two cosmic principles of *yin* and *yang* whose reactions supposedly created all things.

Yü wu: Being and nonbeing.

Selected Bibliography

General Works on Chinese Culture and Philosophy

Bodde, Derk. *China's Cultural Tradition: What and Whither?* New York: Rinehart, 1957.

Chai, Ch'u, and Chai, Winberg. *The Changing Society in China.* New York: The New American Library, to be published in 1961.

Chai, Ch'u. "Chinese Culture: Geographic and Historical Interpretations," *Tsing Hua Journal of Chinese Studies,* V, No. 2, 1961.

———. "Chinese Humanism: A Study of Chinese Mentality and Temperament," *Social Research,* XXVI, No. 1, 1959.

———. "The Spirit of Chinese Culture," *Social Research,* XXIV, No. 1, 1957.

———. "Neo-Confucianism of the Sung-Ming Periods," *Social Research,* XVIII, No. 3, 1951.

Chan, Wing-tsit. *An Outline and an Annotated Bibliography of Chinese Philosophy.* New Haven: Yale University Far Eastern Publications, 1959.

———. *Religious Trends in Modern China.* New York: Columbia University Press, 1953.

Chang, Carsun. *The Development of Neo-Confucian Thought.* New York: Bookman Associates, 1957.

Creel, H. G. *Chinese Thought from Confucius to Mao Tse-tung.* Chicago: University of Chicago Press, 1953.

de Bary, W. Theodore, Chan, Wing-tsit, and Watson, Burton (eds.). *Sources of Chinese Tradition.* New York: Columbia University Press, 1960.

Fairbank, John K. (ed.). *Chinese Thought and Institutions.* Chicago: University of Chicago Press, 1957.

Fung Yu-lan. *A History of Chinese Philosophy,* 2 vols. Translated by Derk Bodde. Princeton: Princeton University Press, 1952, 1953.

―――. *A Short History of Chinese Philosophy.* Edited by Derk Bodde. New York: Macmillan, 1948.

―――. *The Spirit of Chinese Philosophy.* Translated by E. R. Hughes. London: Kegan Paul, 1947.

Giles, Herbert A. *A History of Chinese Literature.* New York and London: D. Appleton, 1927.

Goodrich, Luther Carrington. *A Short History of the Chinese People,* 3rd ed. New York: Harper, 1959.

Hu Shih. *The Chinese Renaissance.* Chicago: University of Chicago Press, 1934.

———. *The Development of The Logical Method in Ancient China*, 3rd ed. Shanghai: Oriental Books, 1928.

Hughes, E. R. *Chinese Philosophy in Classical Times*, rev. ed. London: J. M. Dent, 1954.

Latourette, Kenneth Scott. *The Chinese: Their History and Culture*, 3rd ed., rev. New York: Macmillan, 1946.

Levenson, Joseph R. *Confucian China and Its Modern Fate*. Berkeley: University of California Press, 1958.

Li Chi. *The Beginnings of Chinese Civilization*. Seattle: University of Washington Press, 1957.

Lin Yutang. *The Wisdom of China and India*. New York: Random House, 1942.

Liu Wu-chi. *Confucius, His Life and Time*. New York: Philosophical Library, 1956.

———. *A Short History of Confucian Philosophy*. Harmondsworth: Penguin Books, 1955.

MacNair, Harley F. (ed.). *China*. Berkeley: University of California Press, 1946.

Moore, Charles A. (ed.). *Philosophy—East and West*. Princeton: Princeton University Press, 1944.

Needham, Joseph (with Wang Ling). *Science and Civilization in China*. (*History of Scientific Thought, Vol. II*). Cambridge, Eng.: Cambridge University Press, 1956.

Nivison, David S., and Wright, Arthur F. (eds.). *Confucianism in Action*. Stanford: Stanford University Press, 1959.

Suzuki, D. T. *A Brief History of Chinese Philosophy*. London: Probsthain, 1914.

Waley, Arthur. *Three Ways of Thought in Ancient China*. London: Allen and Unwin, 1939.

Wright, Arthur F. (ed.). *Studies in Chinese Thought*. Chicago: University of Chicago Press, 1953.

Zen, Sophia H. Chen (ed.). *Symposium on Chinese Culture*. Shanghai: China Institute of Pacific Relations, 1931.

Major Classics and Philosophical Works

Basic Writings of Chinese Philosophy, 3 vols. Translated by Ch'u Chai and Winberg Chai. New York: Bantam Books, 1962–64.

    Vol. I, *Basic Writings of Chinese Humanism*, to be published in 1962.

    Vol. II, *Basic Writings of Chinese Naturalism*, to be published in 1963.

    Vol. III, *Basic Writings of Chinese Neo-Humanism*, to be published in 1964.

Chu Hsi. *The Philosophy of Human Nature, by Chu Hsi*. Translated by J. Percy Bruce. London: Probsthain, 1922.

Chuang Tzŭ. *Chuang Tzŭ, A New Selected Transla-*

tion with an Exposition of the Philosophy of Kuo Hsiang. Translated by Fung Yu-lan. Shanghai: Commercial Press, 1933.
The Writings of Chuang Tzŭ. Translated by James Legge, in *The Texts of Taoism*. New York: Julian Press, 1959.

Confucius. *The Analects of Confucius*. Translated by Arthur Waley. London: Allen and Unwin, 1938.
The Wisdom of Confucius. Edited and translated by Lin Yutang. New York: Random House, 1938.
The Great Learning. Translated by James Legge, in *The Chinese Classics,* Vol. I. Oxford, 1893.

Han Fei Tzŭ. *The Complete Works of Han Fei Tzŭ*, Vols. I, II. Translated by W. K. Liao. London: Probsthain, 1939, 1959.

Hsün Tzŭ. *The Works of Hsüntze*. Translated by Homer H. Dubs. London: Probsthain, 1928.

I [*Yi*] *Ching. The I Ching or Book of Changes*. Translated by Cary F. Baynes from the German version of Richard Wilhelm, 2 vols. New York: Pantheon Books, 1950.
The Way and Its Power. Translated by Arthur Waley: London: Allen and Unwin, 1935.
Li Ki (*Chi*), *The Book of Rites*. Translated by James Legge, in *The Sacred Books of the East,* Vols. XXVII, XXVIII. Oxford, 1885.

Lieh Tzŭ. *Taoist Teachings from the Book of Lieh Tzŭ*. Translated by Lionel Giles. London: John Murray, 1912.

Mencius. *The Book of Mencius*. Translated by Lionel Giles. London: John Murray, 1942.
The Works of Mencius. Translated by James Legge. In *The Chinese Classics*, Vol. II. Oxford, 1893.

Mo Tzŭ. *The Ethical and Political Works of Motse*. Translated by Y. P. Mei. London: Probsthain, 1929.

Shang Yang. *The Book of Lord Shang*. Translated by J. J. L. Duyvendak. London: Probsthain, 1928.

Shih Ching, The Book of Odes. Translated by Bernhard Karlgren. Stockholm: Museum of Far Eastern Antiquities, 1950.

Shu Ching, The Book of Documents. Translated by Bernhard Karlgren. Stockholm: Museum of Far Eastern Antiquities, 1950.

Yang Chu. *Yang Chu's Garden of Pleasure*. Translated by Anton Forke. London: John Murray, 1912.